A Midsummer Night's Dream

By Edward de Vere

Art:

Portrait of Edward de Vere
17th Earl of Oxford (1550-1604)

This edition produced by
Verus Publishing

V | P

www.verusbooks.com

ISBN: 978-1-951267-33-9
Imprint / Publisher: Verus Publishing

The Author

Edward de Vere, 17th Earl of Oxford

Biography and Bibliography
After the Play

A Preverse

Drone on ye learned scholars of the day
As to with whom the words ahead the credit lay.
For our part though can be no further doubt
That the author of these words has been found out
To be a person lordly and refined
On whom the light of wit so boldly shined
That to keep this wit from tearing in the fray
He gave another, lesser wit his say.

Now let the least of wits
That writes these paltry lines
Yield to him whose peerless name
Should be with reverence spake.
Let this name be not of history's misassigns
Whose pen and verse have made the earth to shake.

A Midsummer Night's Dream

By Edward de Vere

The Main Characters

Theseus - Duke of Athens

Hippolyta - Queen of the Amazons

Egeus - Father of Hermia

Hermia - Daughter of Egeus, in love with Lysander

Lysander - In love with Hermia

Demetrius - Suitor to Hermia, former lover of Helena

Helena - In love with Demetrius

Philostrate - Master of the Revels

Peter Quince - A Carpenter

Nick Bottom – A Weaver

Francis Flute - A Bellows-mender

Tom Snout - A Tinker

Snug - A Joiner

Robin Starveling - A Tailor

Oberon - King of the Fairies

Titania - Queen of the Fairies

Robin "Puck" Goodfellow - A Mischievous Sprite

Peaseblossom, Cobweb, Moth and
    Mustardseed - Fairy Servants to Titania

Indian changeling - A Ward of Titania

And now, the Play...

ACT I

SCENE I.

Athens. The palace of THESEUS.

*Enter THESEUS, HIPPOLYTA, PHILOSTRATE, and
Attendants*

THESEUS
    Now, fair Hippolyta, our nuptial hour
    Draws on apace; four happy days bring in
    Another moon: but, O, methinks, how slow
    This old moon wanes! she lingers my desires,
    Like to a step-dame or a dowager
    Long withering out a young man revenue.
HIPPOLYTA
    Four days will quickly steep themselves in night;
    Four nights will quickly dream away the time;
    And then the moon, like to a silver bow
    New-bent in heaven, shall behold the night
    Of our solemnities.
THESEUS
    Go, Philostrate,
    Stir up the Athenian youth to merriments;
    Awake the pert and nimble spirit of mirth;
    Turn melancholy forth to funerals;
    The pale companion is not for our pomp.

Exit PHILOSTRATE

    Hippolyta, I woo'd thee with my sword,
    And won thy love, doing thee injuries;
    But I will wed thee in another key,
    With pomp, with triumph and with revelling.

Enter EGEUS, HERMIA, LYSANDER, and DEMETRIUS

EGEUS
   Happy be Theseus, our renowned duke!
THESEUS
   Thanks, good Egeus: what's the news with thee?
EGEUS
   Full of vexation come I, with complaint
   Against my child, my daughter Hermia.
   Stand forth, Demetrius. My noble lord,
   This man hath my consent to marry her.
   Stand forth, Lysander: and my gracious duke,
   This man hath bewitch'd the bosom of my child;
   Thou, thou, Lysander, thou hast given her rhymes,
   And interchanged love-tokens with my child:
   Thou hast by moonlight at her window sung,
   With feigning voice verses of feigning love,
   And stolen the impression of her fantasy
   With bracelets of thy hair, rings, gawds, conceits,
   Knacks, trifles, nosegays, sweetmeats, messengers
   Of strong prevailment in unharden'd youth:
   With cunning hast thou filch'd my daughter's heart,
   Turn'd her obedience, which is due to me,
   To stubborn harshness: and, my gracious duke,
   Be it so she; will not here before your grace
   Consent to marry with Demetrius,
   I beg the ancient privilege of Athens,
   As she is mine, I may dispose of her:
   Which shall be either to this gentleman
   Or to her death, according to our law
   Immediately provided in that case.
THESEUS
   What say you, Hermia? be advised fair maid:
   To you your father should be as a god;

One that composed your beauties, yea, and one
To whom you are but as a form in wax
By him imprinted and within his power
To leave the figure or disfigure it.
Demetrius is a worthy gentleman.

HERMIA

So is Lysander.

THESEUS

In himself he is;
But in this kind, wanting your father's voice,
The other must be held the worthier.

HERMIA

I would my father look'd but with my eyes.

THESEUS

Rather your eyes must with his judgment look.

HERMIA

I do entreat your grace to pardon me.
I know not by what power I am made bold,
Nor how it may concern my modesty,
In such a presence here to plead my thoughts;
But I beseech your grace that I may know
The worst that may befall me in this case,
If I refuse to wed Demetrius.

THESEUS

Either to die the death or to abjure
For ever the society of men.
Therefore, fair Hermia, question your desires;
Know of your youth, examine well your blood,
Whether, if you yield not to your father's choice,
You can endure the livery of a nun,
For aye to be in shady cloister mew'd,
To live a barren sister all your life,
Chanting faint hymns to the cold fruitless moon.
Thrice-blessed they that master so their blood,

To undergo such maiden pilgrimage;
But earthlier happy is the rose distill'd,
Than that which withering on the virgin thorn
Grows, lives and dies in single blessedness.

HERMIA

So will I grow, so live, so die, my lord,
Ere I will my virgin patent up
Unto his lordship, whose unwished yoke
My soul consents not to give sovereignty.

THESEUS

Take time to pause; and, by the next new moon--
The sealing-day betwixt my love and me,
For everlasting bond of fellowship--
Upon that day either prepare to die
For disobedience to your father's will,
Or else to wed Demetrius, as he would;
Or on Diana's altar to protest
For aye austerity and single life.

DEMETRIUS

Relent, sweet Hermia: and, Lysander, yield
Thy crazed title to my certain right.

LYSANDER

You have her father's love, Demetrius;
Let me have Hermia's: do you marry him.

EGEUS

Scornful Lysander! true, he hath my love,
And what is mine my love shall render him.
And she is mine, and all my right of her
I do estate unto Demetrius.

LYSANDER

I am, my lord, as well derived as he,
As well possess'd; my love is more than his;
My fortunes every way as fairly rank'd,
If not with vantage, as Demetrius';

And, which is more than all these boasts can be,
I am beloved of beauteous Hermia:
Why should not I then prosecute my right?
Demetrius, I'll avouch it to his head,
Made love to Nedar's daughter, Helena,
And won her soul; and she, sweet lady, dotes,
Devoutly dotes, dotes in idolatry,
Upon this spotted and inconstant man.

THESEUS
I must confess that I have heard so much,
And with Demetrius thought to have spoke thereof;
But, being over-full of self-affairs,
My mind did lose it. But, Demetrius, come;
And come, Egeus; you shall go with me,
I have some private schooling for you both.
For you, fair Hermia, look you arm yourself
To fit your fancies to your father's will;
Or else the law of Athens yields you up--
Which by no means we may extenuate--
To death, or to a vow of single life.
Come, my Hippolyta: what cheer, my love?
Demetrius and Egeus, go along:
I must employ you in some business
Against our nuptial and confer with you
Of something nearly that concerns yourselves.

EGEUS
With duty and desire we follow you.

Exeunt all but LYSANDER and HERMIA

LYSANDER
How now, my love! why is your cheek so pale?
How chance the roses there do fade so fast?

HERMIA
Belike for want of rain, which I could well

Beteem them from the tempest of my eyes.
LYSANDER
    Ay me! for aught that I could ever read,
    Could ever hear by tale or history,
    The course of true love never did run smooth;
    But, either it was different in blood,--
HERMIA
    O cross! too high to be enthrall'd to low.
LYSANDER
    Or else misgraffed in respect of years,--
HERMIA
    O spite! too old to be engaged to young.
LYSANDER
    Or else it stood upon the choice of friends,--
HERMIA
    O hell! to choose love by another's eyes.
LYSANDER
    Or, if there were a sympathy in choice,
    War, death, or sickness did lay siege to it,
    Making it momentany as a sound,
    Swift as a shadow, short as any dream;
    Brief as the lightning in the collied night,
    That, in a spleen, unfolds both heaven and earth,
    And ere a man hath power to say 'Behold!'
    The jaws of darkness do devour it up:
    So quick bright things come to confusion.
HERMIA
    If then true lovers have been ever cross'd,
    It stands as an edict in destiny:
    Then let us teach our trial patience,
    Because it is a customary cross,
    As due to love as thoughts and dreams and sighs,
    Wishes and tears, poor fancy's followers.
LYSANDER

A good persuasion: therefore, hear me, Hermia.
I have a widow aunt, a dowager
Of great revenue, and she hath no child:
From Athens is her house remote seven leagues;
And she respects me as her only son.
There, gentle Hermia, may I marry thee;
And to that place the sharp Athenian law
Cannot pursue us. If thou lovest me then,
Steal forth thy father's house to-morrow night;
And in the wood, a league without the town,
Where I did meet thee once with Helena,
To do observance to a morn of May,
There will I stay for thee.

HERMIA

My good Lysander!
I swear to thee, by Cupid's strongest bow,
By his best arrow with the golden head,
By the simplicity of Venus' doves,
By that which knitteth souls and prospers loves,
And by that fire which burn'd the Carthage queen,
When the false Troyan under sail was seen,
By all the vows that ever men have broke,
In number more than ever women spoke,
In that same place thou hast appointed me,
To-morrow truly will I meet with thee.

LYSANDER

Keep promise, love. Look, here comes Helena.

Enter HELENA

HERMIA

God speed fair Helena! whither away?

HELENA

Call you me fair? that fair again unsay.
Demetrius loves your fair: O happy fair!
Your eyes are lode-stars; and your tongue's sweet air

More tuneable than lark to shepherd's ear,
When wheat is green, when hawthorn buds appear.
Sickness is catching: O, were favour so,
Yours would I catch, fair Hermia, ere I go;
My ear should catch your voice, my eye your eye,
My tongue should catch your tongue's sweet melody.
Were the world mine, Demetrius being bated,
The rest I'd give to be to you translated.
O, teach me how you look, and with what art
You sway the motion of Demetrius' heart.

HERMIA

I frown upon him, yet he loves me still.

HELENA

O that your frowns would teach my smiles such skill!

HERMIA

I give him curses, yet he gives me love.

HELENA

O that my prayers could such affection move!

HERMIA

The more I hate, the more he follows me.

HELENA

The more I love, the more he hateth me.

HERMIA

His folly, Helena, is no fault of mine.

HELENA

None, but your beauty: would that fault were mine!

HERMIA

Take comfort: he no more shall see my face;
Lysander and myself will fly this place.
Before the time I did Lysander see,
Seem'd Athens as a paradise to me:
O, then, what graces in my love do dwell,
That he hath turn'd a heaven unto a hell!

LYSANDER

Helen, to you our minds we will unfold:
To-morrow night, when Phoebe doth behold
Her silver visage in the watery glass,
Decking with liquid pearl the bladed grass,
A time that lovers' flights doth still conceal,
Through Athens' gates have we devised to steal.

HERMIA

And in the wood, where often you and I
Upon faint primrose-beds were wont to lie,
Emptying our bosoms of their counsel sweet,
There my Lysander and myself shall meet;
And thence from Athens turn away our eyes,
To seek new friends and stranger companies.
Farewell, sweet playfellow: pray thou for us;
And good luck grant thee thy Demetrius!
Keep word, Lysander: we must starve our sight
From lovers' food till morrow deep midnight.

LYSANDER

I will, my Hermia.

Exit HERMIA

Helena, adieu:
As you on him, Demetrius dote on you!

Exit

HELENA

How happy some o'er other some can be!
Through Athens I am thought as fair as she.
But what of that? Demetrius thinks not so;
He will not know what all but he do know:
And as he errs, doting on Hermia's eyes,
So I, admiring of his qualities:
Things base and vile, folding no quantity,
Love can transpose to form and dignity:

Love looks not with the eyes, but with the mind;
And therefore is wing'd Cupid painted blind:
Nor hath Love's mind of any judgement taste;
Wings and no eyes figure unheedy haste:
And therefore is Love said to be a child,
Because in choice he is so oft beguiled.
As waggish boys in game themselves forswear,
So the boy Love is perjured every where:
For ere Demetrius look'd on Hermia's eyne,
He hail'd down oaths that he was only mine;
And when this hail some heat from Hermia felt,
So he dissolved, and showers of oaths did melt.
I will go tell him of fair Hermia's flight:
Then to the wood will he to-morrow night
Pursue her; and for this intelligence
If I have thanks, it is a dear expense:
But herein mean I to enrich my pain,
To have his sight thither and back again.

Exit

SCENE II.

Athens. QUINCE'S house.

*Enter QUINCE, SNUG, BOTTOM, FLUTE, SNOUT, and
STARVELING*

QUINCE
Is all our company here?
BOTTOM
You were best to call them generally, man by man,
according to the scrip.
QUINCE
Here is the scroll of every man's name, which is
thought fit, through all Athens, to play in our
interlude before the duke and the duchess, on his

15

wedding-day at night.

BOTTOM

First, good Peter Quince, say what the play treats
on, then read the names of the actors, and so grow
to a point.

QUINCE

Marry, our play is, The most lamentable comedy, and
most cruel death of Pyramus and Thisby.

BOTTOM

A very good piece of work, I assure you, and a
merry. Now, good Peter Quince, call forth your
actors by the scroll. Masters, spread yourselves.

QUINCE

Answer as I call you. Nick Bottom, the weaver.

BOTTOM

Ready. Name what part I am for, and proceed.

QUINCE

You, Nick Bottom, are set down for Pyramus.

BOTTOM

What is Pyramus? a lover, or a tyrant?

QUINCE

A lover, that kills himself most gallant for love.

BOTTOM

That will ask some tears in the true performing of
it: if I do it, let the audience look to their
eyes; I will move storms, I will condole in some
measure. To the rest: yet my chief humour is for a
tyrant: I could play Ercles rarely, or a part to
tear a cat in, to make all split.
The raging rocks
And shivering shocks
Shall break the locks
Of prison gates;
And Phibbus' car

Shall shine from far
And make and mar
The foolish Fates.
This was lofty! Now name the rest of the players.
This is Ercles' vein, a tyrant's vein; a lover is
more condoling.

QUINCE

Francis Flute, the bellows-mender.

FLUTE

Here, Peter Quince.

QUINCE

Flute, you must take Thisby on you.

FLUTE

What is Thisby? a wandering knight?

QUINCE

It is the lady that Pyramus must love.

FLUTE

Nay, faith, let me not play a woman; I have a beard
coming.

QUINCE

That's all one: you shall play it in a mask, and
you may speak as small as you will.

BOTTOM

An I may hide my face, let me play Thisby too, I'll
speak in a monstrous little voice. 'Thisne,
Thisne;' 'Ah, Pyramus, lover dear! thy Thisby dear,
and lady dear!'

QUINCE

No, no; you must play Pyramus: and, Flute, you Thisby.

BOTTOM

Well, proceed.

QUINCE

Robin Starveling, the tailor.

STARVELING

Here, Peter Quince.
QUINCE
Robin Starveling, you must play Thisby's mother.
Tom Snout, the tinker.
SNOUT
Here, Peter Quince.
QUINCE
You, Pyramus' father: myself, Thisby's father:
Snug, the joiner; you, the lion's part: and, I
hope, here is a play fitted.
SNUG
Have you the lion's part written? pray you, if it
be, give it me, for I am slow of study.
QUINCE
You may do it extempore, for it is nothing but roaring.
BOTTOM
Let me play the lion too: I will roar, that I will
do any man's heart good to hear me; I will roar,
that I will make the duke say 'Let him roar again,
let him roar again.'
QUINCE
An you should do it too terribly, you would fright
the duchess and the ladies, that they would shriek;
and that were enough to hang us all.
ALL
That would hang us, every mother's son.
BOTTOM
I grant you, friends, if that you should fright the
ladies out of their wits, they would have no more
discretion but to hang us: but I will aggravate my
voice so that I will roar you as gently as any
sucking dove; I will roar you an 'twere any
nightingale.
QUINCE

You can play no part but Pyramus; for Pyramus is a
sweet-faced man; a proper man, as one shall see in a
summer's day; a most lovely gentleman-like man:
therefore you must needs play Pyramus.

BOTTOM

Well, I will undertake it. What beard were I best
to play it in?

QUINCE

Why, what you will.

BOTTOM

I will discharge it in either your straw-colour
beard, your orange-tawny beard, your purple-in-grain
beard, or your French-crown-colour beard, your
perfect yellow.

QUINCE

Some of your French crowns have no hair at all, and
then you will play bare-faced. But, masters, here
are your parts: and I am to entreat you, request
you and desire you, to con them by to-morrow night;
and meet me in the palace wood, a mile without the
town, by moonlight; there will we rehearse, for if
we meet in the city, we shall be dogged with
company, and our devices known. In the meantime I
will draw a bill of properties, such as our play
wants. I pray you, fail me not.

BOTTOM

We will meet; and there we may rehearse most
obscenely and courageously. Take pains; be perfect:
adieu.

QUINCE

At the duke's oak we meet.

BOTTOM

Enough; hold or cut bow-strings.

Exeunt

ACT II

SCENE I.

A wood near Athens.

Enter, from opposite sides, a Fairy, and PUCK

PUCK
  How now, spirit! whither wander you?
Fairy
  Over hill, over dale,
  Thorough bush, thorough brier,
  Over park, over pale,
  Thorough flood, thorough fire,
  I do wander everywhere,
  Swifter than the moon's sphere;
  And I serve the fairy queen,
  To dew her orbs upon the green.
  The cowslips tall her pensioners be:
  In their gold coats spots you see;
  Those be rubies, fairy favours,
  In those freckles live their savours:
  I must go seek some dewdrops here
  And hang a pearl in every cowslip's ear.
  Farewell, thou lob of spirits; I'll be gone:
  Our queen and all our elves come here anon.
PUCK
  The king doth keep his revels here to-night:
  Take heed the queen come not within his sight;
  For Oberon is passing fell and wrath,
  Because that she as her attendant hath
  A lovely boy, stolen from an Indian king;
  She never had so sweet a changeling;
  And jealous Oberon would have the child

Knight of his train, to trace the forests wild;
But she perforce withholds the loved boy,
Crowns him with flowers and makes him all her joy:
And now they never meet in grove or green,
By fountain clear, or spangled starlight sheen,
But, they do square, that all their elves for fear
Creep into acorn-cups and hide them there.

Fairy
Either I mistake your shape and making quite,
Or else you are that shrewd and knavish sprite
Call'd Robin Goodfellow: are not you he
That frights the maidens of the villagery;
Skim milk, and sometimes labour in the quern
And bootless make the breathless housewife churn;
And sometime make the drink to bear no barm;
Mislead night-wanderers, laughing at their harm?
Those that Hobgoblin call you and sweet Puck,
You do their work, and they shall have good luck:
Are not you he?

PUCK
Thou speak'st aright;
I am that merry wanderer of the night.
I jest to Oberon and make him smile
When I a fat and bean-fed horse beguile,
Neighing in likeness of a filly foal:
And sometime lurk I in a gossip's bowl,
In very likeness of a roasted crab,
And when she drinks, against her lips I bob
And on her wither'd dewlap pour the ale.
The wisest aunt, telling the saddest tale,
Sometime for three-foot stool mistaketh me;
Then slip I from her bum, down topples she,
And 'tailor' cries, and falls into a cough;
And then the whole quire hold their hips and laugh,

And waxen in their mirth and neeze and swear
A merrier hour was never wasted there.
But, room, fairy! here comes Oberon.
Fairy
And here my mistress. Would that he were gone!

Enter, from one side, OBERON, with his train; from the
other, TITANIA, with hers

OBERON
Ill met by moonlight, proud Titania.
TITANIA
What, jealous Oberon! Fairies, skip hence:
I have forsworn his bed and company.
OBERON
Tarry, rash wanton: am not I thy lord?
TITANIA
Then I must be thy lady: but I know
When thou hast stolen away from fairy land,
And in the shape of Corin sat all day,
Playing on pipes of corn and versing love
To amorous Phillida. Why art thou here,
Come from the farthest Steppe of India?
But that, forsooth, the bouncing Amazon,
Your buskin'd mistress and your warrior love,
To Theseus must be wedded, and you come
To give their bed joy and prosperity.
OBERON
How canst thou thus for shame, Titania,
Glance at my credit with Hippolyta,
Knowing I know thy love to Theseus?
Didst thou not lead him through the glimmering night
From Perigenia, whom he ravished?
And make him with fair AEgle break his faith,
With Ariadne and Antiopa?

22

TITANIA

    These are the forgeries of jealousy:
    And never, since the middle summer's spring,
    Met we on hill, in dale, forest or mead,
    By paved fountain or by rushy brook,
    Or in the beached margent of the sea,
    To dance our ringlets to the whistling wind,
    But with thy brawls thou hast disturb'd our sport.
    Therefore the winds, piping to us in vain,
    As in revenge, have suck'd up from the sea
    Contagious fogs; which falling in the land
    Have every pelting river made so proud
    That they have overborne their continents:
    The ox hath therefore stretch'd his yoke in vain,
    The ploughman lost his sweat, and the green corn
    Hath rotted ere his youth attain'd a beard;
    The fold stands empty in the drowned field,
    And crows are fatted with the murrion flock;
    The nine men's morris is fill'd up with mud,
    And the quaint mazes in the wanton green
    For lack of tread are undistinguishable:
    The human mortals want their winter here;
    No night is now with hymn or carol blest:
    Therefore the moon, the governess of floods,
    Pale in her anger, washes all the air,
    That rheumatic diseases do abound:
    And thorough this distemperature we see
    The seasons alter: hoary-headed frosts
    Far in the fresh lap of the crimson rose,
    And on old Hiems' thin and icy crown
    An odorous chaplet of sweet summer buds
    Is, as in mockery, set: the spring, the summer,
    The childing autumn, angry winter, change
    Their wonted liveries, and the mazed world,

By their increase, now knows not which is which:
And this same progeny of evils comes
From our debate, from our dissension;
We are their parents and original.

OBERON

Do you amend it then; it lies in you:
Why should Titania cross her Oberon?
I do but beg a little changeling boy,
To be my henchman.

TITANIA

Set your heart at rest:
The fairy land buys not the child of me.
His mother was a votaress of my order:
And, in the spiced Indian air, by night,
Full often hath she gossip'd by my side,
And sat with me on Neptune's yellow sands,
Marking the embarked traders on the flood,
When we have laugh'd to see the sails conceive
And grow big-bellied with the wanton wind;
Which she, with pretty and with swimming gait
Following,--her womb then rich with my young
squire,--
Would imitate, and sail upon the land,
To fetch me trifles, and return again,
As from a voyage, rich with merchandise.
But she, being mortal, of that boy did die;
And for her sake do I rear up her boy,
And for her sake I will not part with him.

OBERON

How long within this wood intend you stay?

TITANIA

Perchance till after Theseus' wedding-day.
If you will patiently dance in our round
And see our moonlight revels, go with us;

If not, shun me, and I will spare your haunts.

OBERON

Give me that boy, and I will go with thee.

TITANIA

Not for thy fairy kingdom. Fairies, away!
We shall chide downright, if I longer stay.

Exit TITANIA with her train

OBERON

Well, go thy way: thou shalt not from this grove
Till I torment thee for this injury.
My gentle Puck, come hither. Thou rememberest
Since once I sat upon a promontory,
And heard a mermaid on a dolphin's back
Uttering such dulcet and harmonious breath
That the rude sea grew civil at her song
And certain stars shot madly from their spheres,
To hear the sea-maid's music.

PUCK

I remember.

OBERON

That very time I saw, but thou couldst not,
Flying between the cold moon and the earth,
Cupid all arm'd: a certain aim he took
At a fair vestal throned by the west,
And loosed his love-shaft smartly from his bow,
As it should pierce a hundred thousand hearts;
But I might see young Cupid's fiery shaft
Quench'd in the chaste beams of the watery moon,
And the imperial votaress passed on,
In maiden meditation, fancy-free.
Yet mark'd I where the bolt of Cupid fell:
It fell upon a little western flower,
Before milk-white, now purple with love's wound,

And maidens call it love-in-idleness.
Fetch me that flower; the herb I shew'd thee once:
The juice of it on sleeping eye-lids laid
Will make or man or woman madly dote
Upon the next live creature that it sees.
Fetch me this herb; and be thou here again
Ere the leviathan can swim a league.

PUCK
I'll put a girdle round about the earth
In forty minutes.

Exit

OBERON
Having once this juice,
I'll watch Titania when she is asleep,
And drop the liquor of it in her eyes.
The next thing then she waking looks upon,
Be it on lion, bear, or wolf, or bull,
On meddling monkey, or on busy ape,
She shall pursue it with the soul of love:
And ere I take this charm from off her sight,
As I can take it with another herb,
I'll make her render up her page to me.
But who comes here? I am invisible;
And I will overhear their conference.

Enter DEMETRIUS, HELENA, following him

DEMETRIUS
I love thee not, therefore pursue me not.
Where is Lysander and fair Hermia?
The one I'll slay, the other slayeth me.
Thou told'st me they were stolen unto this wood;
And here am I, and wode within this wood,

26

Because I cannot meet my Hermia.
Hence, get thee gone, and follow me no more.
HELENA
You draw me, you hard-hearted adamant;
But yet you draw not iron, for my heart
Is true as steel: leave you your power to draw,
And I shall have no power to follow you.
DEMETRIUS
Do I entice you? do I speak you fair?
Or, rather, do I not in plainest truth
Tell you, I do not, nor I cannot love you?
HELENA
And even for that do I love you the more.
I am your spaniel; and, Demetrius,
The more you beat me, I will fawn on you:
Use me but as your spaniel, spurn me, strike me,
Neglect me, lose me; only give me leave,
Unworthy as I am, to follow you.
What worser place can I beg in your love,--
And yet a place of high respect with me,--
Than to be used as you use your dog?
DEMETRIUS
Tempt not too much the hatred of my spirit;
For I am sick when I do look on thee.
HELENA
And I am sick when I look not on you.
DEMETRIUS
You do impeach your modesty too much,
To leave the city and commit yourself
Into the hands of one that loves you not;
To trust the opportunity of night
And the ill counsel of a desert place
With the rich worth of your virginity.
HELENA

Your virtue is my privilege: for that
It is not night when I do see your face,
Therefore I think I am not in the night;
Nor doth this wood lack worlds of company,
For you in my respect are all the world:
Then how can it be said I am alone,
When all the world is here to look on me?

DEMETRIUS

I'll run from thee and hide me in the brakes,
And leave thee to the mercy of wild beasts.

HELENA

The wildest hath not such a heart as you.
Run when you will, the story shall be changed:
Apollo flies, and Daphne holds the chase;
The dove pursues the griffin; the mild hind
Makes speed to catch the tiger; bootless speed,
When cowardice pursues and valour flies.

DEMETRIUS

I will not stay thy questions; let me go:
Or, if thou follow me, do not believe
But I shall do thee mischief in the wood.

HELENA

Ay, in the temple, in the town, the field,
You do me mischief. Fie, Demetrius!
Your wrongs do set a scandal on my sex:
We cannot fight for love, as men may do;
We should be wood and were not made to woo.

Exit DEMETRIUS

I'll follow thee and make a heaven of hell,
To die upon the hand I love so well.

Exit

28

OBERON

Fare thee well, nymph: ere he do leave this grove,
Thou shalt fly him and he shall seek thy love.

Re-enter PUCK

Hast thou the flower there? Welcome, wanderer.

PUCK

Ay, there it is.

OBERON

I pray thee, give it me.
I know a bank where the wild thyme blows,
Where oxlips and the nodding violet grows,
Quite over-canopied with luscious woodbine,
With sweet musk-roses and with eglantine:
There sleeps Titania sometime of the night,
Lull'd in these flowers with dances and delight;
And there the snake throws her enamell'd skin,
Weed wide enough to wrap a fairy in:
And with the juice of this I'll streak her eyes,
And make her full of hateful fantasies.
Take thou some of it, and seek through this grove:
A sweet Athenian lady is in love
With a disdainful youth: anoint his eyes;
But do it when the next thing he espies
May be the lady: thou shalt know the man
By the Athenian garments he hath on.
Effect it with some care, that he may prove
More fond on her than she upon her love:
And look thou meet me ere the first cock crow.

PUCK

Fear not, my lord, your servant shall do so.

Exeunt

29

SCENE II.

Another part of the wood.

Enter TITANIA, with her train

TITANIA
    Come, now a roundel and a fairy song;
    Then, for the third part of a minute, hence;
    Some to kill cankers in the musk-rose buds,
    Some war with rere-mice for their leathern wings,
    To make my small elves coats, and some keep back
    The clamorous owl that nightly hoots and wonders
    At our quaint spirits. Sing me now asleep;
    Then to your offices and let me rest.

The Fairies sing

    You spotted snakes with double tongue,
    Thorny hedgehogs, be not seen;
    Newts and blind-worms, do no wrong,
    Come not near our fairy queen.
    Philomel, with melody
    Sing in our sweet lullaby;
    Lulla, lulla, lullaby, lulla, lulla, lullaby:
    Never harm,
    Nor spell nor charm,
    Come our lovely lady nigh;
    So, good night, with lullaby.
    Weaving spiders, come not here;
    Hence, you long-legg'd spinners, hence!
    Beetles black, approach not near;
    Worm nor snail, do no offence.
    Philomel, with melody, & c.
Fairy
    Hence, away! now all is well:
    One aloof stand sentinel.

Exeunt Fairies. TITANIA sleeps

Enter OBERON and squeezes the flower on TITANIA's eyelids

OBERON

    What thou seest when thou dost wake,
    Do it for thy true-love take,
    Love and languish for his sake:
    Be it ounce, or cat, or bear,
    Pard, or boar with bristled hair,
    In thy eye that shall appear
    When thou wakest, it is thy dear:
    Wake when some vile thing is near.

Exit

Enter LYSANDER and HERMIA

LYSANDER

    Fair love, you faint with wandering in the wood;
    And to speak troth, I have forgot our way:
    We'll rest us, Hermia, if you think it good,
    And tarry for the comfort of the day.

HERMIA

    Be it so, Lysander: find you out a bed;
    For I upon this bank will rest my head.

LYSANDER

    One turf shall serve as pillow for us both;
    One heart, one bed, two bosoms and one troth.

HERMIA

    Nay, good Lysander; for my sake, my dear,
    Lie further off yet, do not lie so near.

LYSANDER

O, take the sense, sweet, of my innocence!
Love takes the meaning in love's conference.
I mean, that my heart unto yours is knit
So that but one heart we can make of it;
Two bosoms interchained with an oath;
So then two bosoms and a single troth.
Then by your side no bed-room me deny;
For lying so, Hermia, I do not lie.

HERMIA

Lysander riddles very prettily:
Now much beshrew my manners and my pride,
If Hermia meant to say Lysander lied.
But, gentle friend, for love and courtesy
Lie further off; in human modesty,
Such separation as may well be said
Becomes a virtuous bachelor and a maid,
So far be distant; and, good night, sweet friend:
Thy love ne'er alter till thy sweet life end!

LYSANDER

Amen, amen, to that fair prayer, say I;
And then end life when I end loyalty!
Here is my bed: sleep give thee all his rest!

HERMIA

With half that wish the wisher's eyes be press'd!

They sleep

Enter PUCK

PUCK

Through the forest have I gone.
But Athenian found I none,
On whose eyes I might approve
This flower's force in stirring love.

32

Night and silence.--Who is here?
Weeds of Athens he doth wear:
This is he, my master said,
Despised the Athenian maid;
And here the maiden, sleeping sound,
On the dank and dirty ground.
Pretty soul! she durst not lie
Near this lack-love, this kill-courtesy.
Churl, upon thy eyes I throw
All the power this charm doth owe.
When thou wakest, let love forbid
Sleep his seat on thy eyelid:
So awake when I am gone;
For I must now to Oberon.

Exit

Enter DEMETRIUS and HELENA, running

HELENA
Stay, though thou kill me, sweet Demetrius.
DEMETRIUS
I charge thee, hence, and do not haunt me thus.
HELENA
O, wilt thou darkling leave me? do not so.
DEMETRIUS
Stay, on thy peril: I alone will go.

Exit

HELENA
O, I am out of breath in this fond chase!
The more my prayer, the lesser is my grace.
Happy is Hermia, wheresoe'er she lies;
For she hath blessed and attractive eyes.

33

How came her eyes so bright? Not with salt tears:
If so, my eyes are oftener wash'd than hers.
No, no, I am as ugly as a bear;
For beasts that meet me run away for fear:
Therefore no marvel though Demetrius
Do, as a monster fly my presence thus.
What wicked and dissembling glass of mine
Made me compare with Hermia's sphery eyne?
But who is here? Lysander! on the ground!
Dead? or asleep? I see no blood, no wound.
Lysander if you live, good sir, awake.

LYSANDER
[Awaking] And run through fire I will for thy sweet
sake.
Transparent Helena! Nature shows art,
That through thy bosom makes me see thy heart.
Where is Demetrius? O, how fit a word
Is that vile name to perish on my sword!

HELENA
Do not say so, Lysander; say not so
What though he love your Hermia? Lord, what though?
Yet Hermia still loves you: then be content.

LYSANDER
Content with Hermia! No; I do repent
The tedious minutes I with her have spent.
Not Hermia but Helena I love:
Who will not change a raven for a dove?
The will of man is by his reason sway'd;
And reason says you are the worthier maid.
Things growing are not ripe until their season
So I, being young, till now ripe not to reason;
And touching now the point of human skill,
Reason becomes the marshal to my will
And leads me to your eyes, where I o'erlook

34

Love's stories written in love's richest book.

HELENA

    Wherefore was I to this keen mockery born?
    When at your hands did I deserve this scorn?
    Is't not enough, is't not enough, young man,
    That I did never, no, nor never can,
    Deserve a sweet look from Demetrius' eye,
    But you must flout my insufficiency?
    Good troth, you do me wrong, good sooth, you do,
    In such disdainful manner me to woo.
    But fare you well: perforce I must confess
    I thought you lord of more true gentleness.
    O, that a lady, of one man refused.
    Should of another therefore be abused!

Exit

LYSANDER

    She sees not Hermia. Hermia, sleep thou there:
    And never mayst thou come Lysander near!
    For as a surfeit of the sweetest things
    The deepest loathing to the stomach brings,
    Or as tie heresies that men do leave
    Are hated most of those they did deceive,
    So thou, my surfeit and my heresy,
    Of all be hated, but the most of me!
    And, all my powers, address your love and might
    To honour Helen and to be her knight!

Exit

HERMIA

    [Awaking] Help me, Lysander, help me! do thy best
    To pluck this crawling serpent from my breast!
    Ay me, for pity! what a dream was here!

Lysander, look how I do quake with fear:
Methought a serpent eat my heart away,
And you sat smiling at his cruel pray.
Lysander! what, removed? Lysander! lord!
What, out of hearing? gone? no sound, no word?
Alack, where are you speak, an if you hear;
Speak, of all loves! I swoon almost with fear.
No? then I well perceive you all not nigh
Either death or you I'll find immediately.

Exit

ACT III

SCENE I.

The wood. TITANIA lying asleep.

Enter QUINCE, SNUG, BOTTOM, FLUTE, SNOUT, and STARVELING

BOTTOM
Are we all met?
QUINCE
Pat, pat; and here's a marvellous convenient place
for our rehearsal. This green plot shall be our
stage, this hawthorn-brake our tiring-house; and we
will do it in action as we will do it before the duke.
BOTTOM
Peter Quince,--
QUINCE
What sayest thou, bully Bottom?
BOTTOM
There are things in this comedy of Pyramus and
Thisby that will never please. First, Pyramus must
draw a sword to kill himself; which the ladies
cannot abide. How answer you that?
SNOUT
By'r lakin, a parlous fear.
STARVELING
I believe we must leave the killing out, when all is done.
BOTTOM
Not a whit: I have a device to make all well.
Write me a prologue; and let the prologue seem to
say, we will do no harm with our swords, and that
Pyramus is not killed indeed; and, for the more
better assurance, tell them that I, Pyramus, am not

Pyramus, but Bottom the weaver: this will put them
out of fear.

QUINCE

Well, we will have such a prologue; and it shall be
written in eight and six.

BOTTOM

No, make it two more; let it be written in eight and
eight.

SNOUT

Will not the ladies be afeard of the lion?

STARVELING

I fear it, I promise you.

BOTTOM

Masters, you ought to consider with yourselves: to
bring in--God shield us!--a lion among ladies, is a
most dreadful thing; for there is not a more fearful
wild-fowl than your lion living; and we ought to
look to 't.

SNOUT

Therefore another prologue must tell he is not a lion.

BOTTOM

Nay, you must name his name, and half his face must
be seen through the lion's neck: and he himself
must speak through, saying thus, or to the same
defect,--'Ladies,'--or 'Fair-ladies--I would wish
You,'--or 'I would request you,'--or 'I would
entreat you,--not to fear, not to tremble: my life
for yours. If you think I come hither as a lion, it
were pity of my life: no I am no such thing; I am a
man as other men are;' and there indeed let him name
his name, and tell them plainly he is Snug the joiner.

QUINCE

Well it shall be so. But there is two hard things;
that is, to bring the moonlight into a chamber; for,

you know, Pyramus and Thisby meet by moonlight.

SNOUT

Doth the moon shine that night we play our play?

BOTTOM

A calendar, a calendar! look in the almanac; find
out moonshine, find out moonshine.

QUINCE

Yes, it doth shine that night.

BOTTOM

Why, then may you leave a casement of the great
chamber window, where we play, open, and the moon
may shine in at the casement.

QUINCE

Ay; or else one must come in with a bush of thorns
and a lanthorn, and say he comes to disfigure, or to
present, the person of Moonshine. Then, there is
another thing: we must have a wall in the great
chamber; for Pyramus and Thisby says the story, did
talk through the chink of a wall.

SNOUT

You can never bring in a wall. What say you, Bottom?

BOTTOM

Some man or other must present Wall: and let him
have some plaster, or some loam, or some rough-cast
about him, to signify wall; and let him hold his
fingers thus, and through that cranny shall Pyramus
and Thisby whisper.

QUINCE

If that may be, then all is well. Come, sit down,
every mother's son, and rehearse your parts.
Pyramus, you begin: when you have spoken your
speech, enter into that brake: and so every one
according to his cue.

Enter PUCK behind

PUCK
    What hempen home-spuns have we swaggering here,
    So near the cradle of the fairy queen?
    What, a play toward! I'll be an auditor;
    An actor too, perhaps, if I see cause.
QUINCE
    Speak, Pyramus. Thisby, stand forth.
BOTTOM
    Thisby, the flowers of odious savours sweet,--
QUINCE
    Odours, odours.
BOTTOM
    --odours savours sweet:
    So hath thy breath, my dearest Thisby dear.
    But hark, a voice! stay thou but here awhile,
    And by and by I will to thee appear.

Exit

PUCK
    A stranger Pyramus than e'er played here.

Exit

FLUTE
    Must I speak now?
QUINCE
    Ay, marry, must you; for you must understand he goes
    but to see a noise that he heard, and is to come again.
FLUTE
    Most radiant Pyramus, most lily-white of hue,
    Of colour like the red rose on triumphant brier,
    Most brisky juvenal and eke most lovely Jew,
    As true as truest horse that yet would never tire,

I'll meet thee, Pyramus, at Ninny's tomb.

QUINCE

'Ninus' tomb,' man: why, you must not speak that
yet; that you answer to Pyramus: you speak all your
part at once, cues and all Pyramus enter: your cue
is past; it is, 'never tire.'

FLUTE

O,--As true as truest horse, that yet would
never tire.

Re-enter PUCK, and BOTTOM with an ass's head

BOTTOM

If I were fair, Thisby, I were only thine.

QUINCE

O monstrous! O strange! we are haunted. Pray,
masters! fly, masters! Help!

Exeunt QUINCE, SNUG, FLUTE, SNOUT, and
STARVELING

PUCK

I'll follow you, I'll lead you about a round,
Through bog, through bush, through brake, through
brier:
Sometime a horse I'll be, sometime a hound,
A hog, a headless bear, sometime a fire;
And neigh, and bark, and grunt, and roar, and burn,
Like horse, hound, hog, bear, fire, at every turn.

Exit

BOTTOM

Why do they run away? this is a knavery of them to
make me afeard.

Re-enter SNOUT

SNOUT
O Bottom, thou art changed! what do I see on thee?
BOTTOM
What do you see? you see an asshead of your own, do
you?

Exit SNOUT

Re-enter QUINCE

QUINCE
Bless thee, Bottom! bless thee! thou art
translated.

Exit

BOTTOM
I see their knavery: this is to make an ass of me;
to fright me, if they could. But I will not stir
from this place, do what they can: I will walk up
and down here, and I will sing, that they shall hear
I am not afraid.

Sings

The ousel cock so black of hue,
With orange-tawny bill,
The throstle with his note so true,
The wren with little quill,--
TITANIA
[Awaking] What angel wakes me from my flowery bed?
BOTTOM
[Sings]
The finch, the sparrow and the lark,
The plain-song cuckoo gray,

42

Whose note full many a man doth mark,
And dares not answer nay;--
for, indeed, who would set his wit to so foolish
a bird? who would give a bird the lie, though he cry
'cuckoo' never so?

TITANIA

I pray thee, gentle mortal, sing again:
Mine ear is much enamour'd of thy note;
So is mine eye enthralled to thy shape;
And thy fair virtue's force perforce doth move me
On the first view to say, to swear, I love thee.

BOTTOM

Methinks, mistress, you should have little reason
for that: and yet, to say the truth, reason and
love keep little company together now-a-days; the
more the pity that some honest neighbours will not
make them friends. Nay, I can gleek upon occasion.

TITANIA

Thou art as wise as thou art beautiful.

BOTTOM

Not so, neither: but if I had wit enough to get out
of this wood, I have enough to serve mine own turn.

TITANIA

Out of this wood do not desire to go:
Thou shalt remain here, whether thou wilt or no.
I am a spirit of no common rate;
The summer still doth tend upon my state;
And I do love thee: therefore, go with me;
I'll give thee fairies to attend on thee,
And they shall fetch thee jewels from the deep,
And sing while thou on pressed flowers dost sleep;
And I will purge thy mortal grossness so
That thou shalt like an airy spirit go.
Peaseblossom! Cobweb! Moth! and Mustardseed!

Enter PEASEBLOSSOM, COBWEB, MOTH, and
MUSTARDSEED

PEASEBLOSSOM
Ready.
COBWEB
And I.
MOTH
And I.
MUSTARDSEED
And I.
ALL
Where shall we go?
TITANIA
Be kind and courteous to this gentleman;
Hop in his walks and gambol in his eyes;
Feed him with apricocks and dewberries,
With purple grapes, green figs, and mulberries;
The honey-bags steal from the humble-bees,
And for night-tapers crop their waxen thighs
And light them at the fiery glow-worm's eyes,
To have my love to bed and to arise;
And pluck the wings from Painted butterflies
To fan the moonbeams from his sleeping eyes:
Nod to him, elves, and do him courtesies.
PEASEBLOSSOM
Hail, mortal!
COBWEB
Hail!
MOTH
Hail!
MUSTARDSEED
Hail!
BOTTOM

I cry your worship's mercy, heartily: I beseech your
worship's name.

COBWEB

Cobweb.

BOTTOM

I shall desire you of more acquaintance, good Master
Cobweb: if I cut my finger, I shall make bold with
you. Your name, honest gentleman?

PEASEBLOSSOM

Peaseblossom.

BOTTOM

I pray you, commend me to Mistress Squash, your
mother, and to Master Peascod, your father. Good
Master Peaseblossom, I shall desire you of more
acquaintance too. Your name, I beseech you, sir?

MUSTARDSEED

Mustardseed.

BOTTOM

Good Master Mustardseed, I know your patience well:
that same cowardly, giant-like ox-beef hath
devoured many a gentleman of your house: I promise
you your kindred had made my eyes water ere now. I
desire your more acquaintance, good Master
Mustardseed.

TITANIA

Come, wait upon him; lead him to my bower.
The moon methinks looks with a watery eye;
And when she weeps, weeps every little flower,
Lamenting some enforced chastity.
Tie up my love's tongue bring him silently.

Exeunt

45

SCENE II.

Another part of the wood.

Enter OBERON

OBERON
  I wonder if Titania be awaked;
  Then, what it was that next came in her eye,
  Which she must dote on in extremity.

Enter PUCK

  Here comes my messenger.
  How now, mad spirit!
  What night-rule now about this haunted grove?
PUCK
  My mistress with a monster is in love.
  Near to her close and consecrated bower,
  While she was in her dull and sleeping hour,
  A crew of patches, rude mechanicals,
  That work for bread upon Athenian stalls,
  Were met together to rehearse a play
  Intended for great Theseus' nuptial-day.
  The shallowest thick-skin of that barren sort,
  Who Pyramus presented, in their sport
  Forsook his scene and enter'd in a brake
  When I did him at this advantage take,
  An ass's nole I fixed on his head:
  Anon his Thisbe must be answered,
  And forth my mimic comes. When they him spy,
  As wild geese that the creeping fowler eye,
  Or russet-pated choughs, many in sort,
  Rising and cawing at the gun's report,
  Sever themselves and madly sweep the sky,
  So, at his sight, away his fellows fly;
  And, at our stamp, here o'er and o'er one falls;

46

He murder cries and help from Athens calls.
Their sense thus weak, lost with their fears
thus strong,
Made senseless things begin to do them wrong;
For briers and thorns at their apparel snatch;
Some sleeves, some hats, from yielders all
things catch.
I led them on in this distracted fear,
And left sweet Pyramus translated there:
When in that moment, so it came to pass,
Titania waked and straightway loved an ass.
OBERON
This falls out better than I could devise.
But hast thou yet latch'd the Athenian's eyes
With the love-juice, as I did bid thee do?
PUCK
I took him sleeping,--that is finish'd too,--
And the Athenian woman by his side:
That, when he waked, of force she must be eyed.

Enter HERMIA and DEMETRIUS

OBERON
Stand close: this is the same Athenian.
PUCK
This is the woman, but not this the man.
DEMETRIUS
O, why rebuke you him that loves you so?
Lay breath so bitter on your bitter foe.
HERMIA
Now I but chide; but I should use thee worse,
For thou, I fear, hast given me cause to curse,
If thou hast slain Lysander in his sleep,
Being o'er shoes in blood, plunge in the deep,
And kill me too.

The sun was not so true unto the day
As he to me: would he have stolen away
From sleeping Hermia? I'll believe as soon
This whole earth may be bored and that the moon
May through the centre creep and so displease
Her brother's noontide with Antipodes.
It cannot be but thou hast murder'd him;
So should a murderer look, so dead, so grim.
DEMETRIUS
So should the murder'd look, and so should I,
Pierced through the heart with your stern cruelty:
Yet you, the murderer, look as bright, as clear,
As yonder Venus in her glimmering sphere.
HERMIA
What's this to my Lysander? where is he?
Ah, good Demetrius, wilt thou give him me?
DEMETRIUS
I had rather give his carcass to my hounds.
HERMIA
Out, dog! out, cur! thou drivest me past the bounds
Of maiden's patience. Hast thou slain him, then?
Henceforth be never number'd among men!
O, once tell true, tell true, even for my sake!
Durst thou have look'd upon him being awake,
And hast thou kill'd him sleeping? O brave touch!
Could not a worm, an adder, do so much?
An adder did it; for with doubler tongue
Than thine, thou serpent, never adder stung.
DEMETRIUS
You spend your passion on a misprised mood:
I am not guilty of Lysander's blood;
Nor is he dead, for aught that I can tell.
HERMIA
I pray thee, tell me then that he is well.

DEMETRIUS
    An if I could, what should I get therefore?
HERMIA
    A privilege never to see me more.
    And from thy hated presence part I so:
    See me no more, whether he be dead or no.

Exit

DEMETRIUS
    There is no following her in this fierce vein:
    Here therefore for a while I will remain
    So sorrow's heaviness doth heavier grow
    For debt that bankrupt sleep doth sorrow owe:
    Which now in some slight measure it will pay,
    If for his tender here I make some stay.

Lies down and sleeps

OBERON
    What hast thou done? thou hast mistaken quite
    And laid the love-juice on some true-love's sight:
    Of thy misprision must perforce ensue
    Some true love turn'd and not a false turn'd true.
PUCK
    Then fate o'er-rules, that, one man holding troth,
    A million fail, confounding oath on oath.
OBERON
    About the wood go swifter than the wind,
    And Helena of Athens look thou find:
    All fancy-sick she is and pale of cheer,
    With sighs of love, that costs the fresh blood dear:
    By some illusion see thou bring her here:
    I'll charm his eyes against she do appear.
PUCK

I go, I go; look how I go,
Swifter than arrow from the Tartar's bow.

Exit

OBERON
Flower of this purple dye,
Hit with Cupid's archery,
Sink in apple of his eye.
When his love he doth espy,
Let her shine as gloriously
As the Venus of the sky.
When thou wakest, if she be by,
Beg of her for remedy.

Re-enter PUCK

PUCK
Captain of our fairy band,
Helena is here at hand;
And the youth, mistook by me,
Pleading for a lover's fee.
Shall we their fond pageant see?
Lord, what fools these mortals be!
OBERON
Stand aside: the noise they make
Will cause Demetrius to awake.
PUCK
Then will two at once woo one;
That must needs be sport alone;
And those things do best please me
That befal preposterously.

Enter LYSANDER and HELENA

LYSANDER

Why should you think that I should woo in scorn?
Scorn and derision never come in tears:
Look, when I vow, I weep; and vows so born,
In their nativity all truth appears.
How can these things in me seem scorn to you,
Bearing the badge of faith, to prove them true?
HELENA
You do advance your cunning more and more.
When truth kills truth, O devilish-holy fray!
These vows are Hermia's: will you give her o'er?
Weigh oath with oath, and you will nothing weigh:
Your vows to her and me, put in two scales,
Will even weigh, and both as light as tales.
LYSANDER
I had no judgment when to her I swore.
HELENA
Nor none, in my mind, now you give her o'er.
LYSANDER
Demetrius loves her, and he loves not you.
DEMETRIUS
[Awaking] O Helena, goddess, nymph, perfect, divine!
To what, my love, shall I compare thine eyne?
Crystal is muddy. O, how ripe in show
Thy lips, those kissing cherries, tempting grow!
That pure congealed white, high Taurus snow,
Fann'd with the eastern wind, turns to a crow
When thou hold'st up thy hand: O, let me kiss
This princess of pure white, this seal of bliss!
HELENA
O spite! O hell! I see you all are bent
To set against me for your merriment:
If you we re civil and knew courtesy,
You would not do me thus much injury.
Can you not hate me, as I know you do,

51

But you must join in souls to mock me too?
If you were men, as men you are in show,
You would not use a gentle lady so;
To vow, and swear, and superpraise my parts,
When I am sure you hate me with your hearts.
You both are rivals, and love Hermia;
And now both rivals, to mock Helena:
A trim exploit, a manly enterprise,
To conjure tears up in a poor maid's eyes
With your derision! none of noble sort
Would so offend a virgin, and extort
A poor soul's patience, all to make you sport.
LYSANDER
You are unkind, Demetrius; be not so;
For you love Hermia; this you know I know:
And here, with all good will, with all my heart,
In Hermia's love I yield you up my part;
And yours of Helena to me bequeath,
Whom I do love and will do till my death.
HELENA
Never did mockers waste more idle breath.
DEMETRIUS
Lysander, keep thy Hermia; I will none:
If e'er I loved her, all that love is gone.
My heart to her but as guest-wise sojourn'd,
And now to Helen is it home return'd,
There to remain.
LYSANDER
Helen, it is not so.
DEMETRIUS
Disparage not the faith thou dost not know,
Lest, to thy peril, thou aby it dear.
Look, where thy love comes; yonder is thy dear.

Re-enter HERMIA

HERMIA
    Dark night, that from the eye his function takes,
    The ear more quick of apprehension makes;
    Wherein it doth impair the seeing sense,
    It pays the hearing double recompense.
    Thou art not by mine eye, Lysander, found;
    Mine ear, I thank it, brought me to thy sound
    But why unkindly didst thou leave me so?
LYSANDER
    Why should he stay, whom love doth press to go?
HERMIA
    What love could press Lysander from my side?
LYSANDER
    Lysander's love, that would not let him bide,
    Fair Helena, who more engilds the night
    Than all you fiery oes and eyes of light.
    Why seek'st thou me? could not this make thee know,
    The hate I bear thee made me leave thee so?
HERMIA
    You speak not as you think: it cannot be.
HELENA
    Lo, she is one of this confederacy!
    Now I perceive they have conjoin'd all three
    To fashion this false sport, in spite of me.
    Injurious Hermia! most ungrateful maid!
    Have you conspired, have you with these contrived
    To bait me with this foul derision?
    Is all the counsel that we two have shared,
    The sisters' vows, the hours that we have spent,
    When we have chid the hasty-footed time
    For parting us,--O, is it all forgot?
    All school-days' friendship, childhood innocence?
    We, Hermia, like two artificial gods,

Have with our needles created both one flower,
Both on one sampler, sitting on one cushion,
Both warbling of one song, both in one key,
As if our hands, our sides, voices and minds,
Had been incorporate. So we grow together,
Like to a double cherry, seeming parted,
But yet an union in partition;
Two lovely berries moulded on one stem;
So, with two seeming bodies, but one heart;
Two of the first, like coats in heraldry,
Due but to one and crowned with one crest.
And will you rent our ancient love asunder,
To join with men in scorning your poor friend?
It is not friendly, 'tis not maidenly:
Our sex, as well as I, may chide you for it,
Though I alone do feel the injury.

HERMIA

I am amazed at your passionate words.
I scorn you not: it seems that you scorn me.

HELENA

Have you not set Lysander, as in scorn,
To follow me and praise my eyes and face?
And made your other love, Demetrius,
Who even but now did spurn me with his foot,
To call me goddess, nymph, divine and rare,
Precious, celestial? Wherefore speaks he this
To her he hates? and wherefore doth Lysander
Deny your love, so rich within his soul,
And tender me, forsooth, affection,
But by your setting on, by your consent?
What thought I be not so in grace as you,
So hung upon with love, so fortunate,
But miserable most, to love unloved?
This you should pity rather than despise.

HERMIA

I understand not what you mean by this.

HELENA

Ay, do, persever, counterfeit sad looks,
Make mouths upon me when I turn my back;
Wink each at other; hold the sweet jest up:
This sport, well carried, shall be chronicled.
If you have any pity, grace, or manners,
You would not make me such an argument.
But fare ye well: 'tis partly my own fault;
Which death or absence soon shall remedy.

LYSANDER

Stay, gentle Helena; hear my excuse:
My love, my life my soul, fair Helena!

HELENA

O excellent!

HERMIA

Sweet, do not scorn her so.

DEMETRIUS

If she cannot entreat, I can compel.

LYSANDER

Thou canst compel no more than she entreat:
Thy threats have no more strength than her weak
prayers.
Helen, I love thee; by my life, I do:
I swear by that which I will lose for thee,
To prove him false that says I love thee not.

DEMETRIUS

I say I love thee more than he can do.

LYSANDER

If thou say so, withdraw, and prove it too.

DEMETRIUS

Quick, come!

HERMIA

Lysander, whereto tends all this?

LYSANDER

Away, you Ethiope!

DEMETRIUS

No, no; he'll [ ]

Seem to break loose; take on as you would follow,

But yet come not: you are a tame man, go!

LYSANDER

Hang off, thou cat, thou burr! vile thing, let loose,

Or I will shake thee from me like a serpent!

HERMIA

Why are you grown so rude? what change is this?

Sweet love,--

LYSANDER

Thy love! out, tawny Tartar, out!

Out, loathed medicine! hated potion, hence!

HERMIA

Do you not jest?

HELENA

Yes, sooth; and so do you.

LYSANDER

Demetrius, I will keep my word with thee.

DEMETRIUS

I would I had your bond, for I perceive

A weak bond holds you: I'll not trust your word.

LYSANDER

What, should I hurt her, strike her, kill her dead?

Although I hate her, I'll not harm her so.

HERMIA

What, can you do me greater harm than hate?

Hate me! wherefore? O me! what news, my love!

Am not I Hermia? are not you Lysander?

I am as fair now as I was erewhile.

Since night you loved me; yet since night you left

me:
Why, then you left me--O, the gods forbid!--
In earnest, shall I say?

LYSANDER

Ay, by my life;
And never did desire to see thee more.
Therefore be out of hope, of question, of doubt;
Be certain, nothing truer; 'tis no jest
That I do hate thee and love Helena.

HERMIA

O me! you juggler! you canker-blossom!
You thief of love! what, have you come by night
And stolen my love's heart from him?

HELENA

Fine, i'faith!
Have you no modesty, no maiden shame,
No touch of bashfulness? What, will you tear
Impatient answers from my gentle tongue?
Fie, fie! you counterfeit, you puppet, you!

HERMIA

Puppet? why so? ay, that way goes the game.
Now I perceive that she hath made compare
Between our statures; she hath urged her height;
And with her personage, her tall personage,
Her height, forsooth, she hath prevail'd with him.
And are you grown so high in his esteem;
Because I am so dwarfish and so low?
How low am I, thou painted maypole? speak;
How low am I? I am not yet so low
But that my nails can reach unto thine eyes.

HELENA

I pray you, though you mock me, gentlemen,
Let her not hurt me: I was never curst;
I have no gift at all in shrewishness;

I am a right maid for my cowardice:
Let her not strike me. You perhaps may think,
Because she is something lower than myself,
That I can match her.

HERMIA

Lower! hark, again.

HELENA

Good Hermia, do not be so bitter with me.
I evermore did love you, Hermia,
Did ever keep your counsels, never wrong'd you;
Save that, in love unto Demetrius,
I told him of your stealth unto this wood.
He follow'd you; for love I follow'd him;
But he hath chid me hence and threaten'd me
To strike me, spurn me, nay, to kill me too:
And now, so you will let me quiet go,
To Athens will I bear my folly back
And follow you no further: let me go:
You see how simple and how fond I am.

HERMIA

Why, get you gone: who is't that hinders you?

HELENA

A foolish heart, that I leave here behind.

HERMIA

What, with Lysander?

HELENA

With Demetrius.

LYSANDER

Be not afraid; she shall not harm thee, Helena.

DEMETRIUS

No, sir, she shall not, though you take her part.

HELENA

O, when she's angry, she is keen and shrewd!
She was a vixen when she went to school;

And though she be but little, she is fierce.

HERMIA

'Little' again! nothing but 'low' and 'little'!
Why will you suffer her to flout me thus?
Let me come to her.

LYSANDER

Get you gone, you dwarf;
You minimus, of hindering knot-grass made;
You bead, you acorn.

DEMETRIUS

You are too officious
In her behalf that scorns your services.
Let her alone: speak not of Helena;
Take not her part; for, if thou dost intend
Never so little show of love to her,
Thou shalt aby it.

LYSANDER

Now she holds me not;
Now follow, if thou darest, to try whose right,
Of thine or mine, is most in Helena.

DEMETRIUS

Follow! nay, I'll go with thee, cheek by jole.

Exeunt LYSANDER and DEMETRIUS

HERMIA

You, mistress, all this coil is 'long of you:
Nay, go not back.

HELENA

I will not trust you, I,
Nor longer stay in your curst company.
Your hands than mine are quicker for a fray,
My legs are longer though, to run away.

Exit

HERMIA
  I am amazed, and know not what to say.

  Exit

OBERON
  This is thy negligence: still thou mistakest,
  Or else committ'st thy knaveries wilfully.
PUCK
  Believe me, king of shadows, I mistook.
  Did not you tell me I should know the man
  By the Athenian garment he had on?
  And so far blameless proves my enterprise,
  That I have 'nointed an Athenian's eyes;
  And so far am I glad it so did sort
  As this their jangling I esteem a sport.
OBERON
  Thou see'st these lovers seek a place to fight:
  Hie therefore, Robin, overcast the night;
  The starry welkin cover thou anon
  With drooping fog as black as Acheron,
  And lead these testy rivals so astray
  As one come not within another's way.
  Like to Lysander sometime frame thy tongue,
  Then stir Demetrius up with bitter wrong;
  And sometime rail thou like Demetrius;
  And from each other look thou lead them thus,
  Till o'er their brows death-counterfeiting sleep
  With leaden legs and batty wings doth creep:
  Then crush this herb into Lysander's eye;
  Whose liquor hath this virtuous property,
  To take from thence all error with his might,
  And make his eyeballs roll with wonted sight.
  When they next wake, all this derision

Shall seem a dream and fruitless vision,
And back to Athens shall the lovers wend,
With league whose date till death shall never end.
Whiles I in this affair do thee employ,
I'll to my queen and beg her Indian boy;
And then I will her charmed eye release
From monster's view, and all things shall be peace.

PUCK
My fairy lord, this must be done with haste,
For night's swift dragons cut the clouds full fast,
And yonder shines Aurora's harbinger;
At whose approach, ghosts, wandering here and there,
Troop home to churchyards: damned spirits all,
That in crossways and floods have burial,
Already to their wormy beds are gone;
For fear lest day should look their shames upon,
They willfully themselves exile from light
And must for aye consort with black-brow'd night.

OBERON
But we are spirits of another sort:
I with the morning's love have oft made sport,
And, like a forester, the groves may tread,
Even till the eastern gate, all fiery-red,
Opening on Neptune with fair blessed beams,
Turns into yellow gold his salt green streams.
But, notwithstanding, haste; make no delay:
We may effect this business yet ere day.

Exit

PUCK
Up and down, up and down,
I will lead them up and down:
I am fear'd in field and town:
Goblin, lead them up and down.

Here comes one.

Re-enter LYSANDER

LYSANDER
Where art thou, proud Demetrius? speak thou now.
PUCK
Here, villain; drawn and ready. Where art thou?
LYSANDER
I will be with thee straight.
PUCK
Follow me, then,
To plainer ground.

Exit LYSANDER, as following the voice

Re-enter DEMETRIUS

DEMETRIUS
Lysander! speak again:
Thou runaway, thou coward, art thou fled?
Speak! In some bush? Where dost thou hide thy head?
PUCK
Thou coward, art thou bragging to the stars,
Telling the bushes that thou look'st for wars,
And wilt not come? Come, recreant; come, thou child;
I'll whip thee with a rod: he is defiled
That draws a sword on thee.
DEMETRIUS
Yea, art thou there?
PUCK
Follow my voice: we'll try no manhood here.

Exeunt

Re-enter LYSANDER

LYSANDER
  He goes before me and still dares me on:
  When I come where he calls, then he is gone.
  The villain is much lighter-heel'd than I:
  I follow'd fast, but faster he did fly;
  That fallen am I in dark uneven way,
  And here will rest me.

Lies down

  Come, thou gentle day!
  For if but once thou show me thy grey light,
  I'll find Demetrius and revenge this spite.

Sleeps

Re-enter PUCK and DEMETRIUS

PUCK
  Ho, ho, ho! Coward, why comest thou not?
DEMETRIUS
  Abide me, if thou darest; for well I wot
  Thou runn'st before me, shifting every place,
  And darest not stand, nor look me in the face.
  Where art thou now?
PUCK
  Come hither: I am here.
DEMETRIUS
  Nay, then, thou mock'st me. Thou shalt buy this dear,
  If ever I thy face by daylight see:
  Now, go thy way. Faintness constraineth me
  To measure out my length on this cold bed.
  By day's approach look to be visited.

Lies down and sleeps

Re-enter HELENA

HELENA
    O weary night, O long and tedious night,
    Abate thy hour! Shine comforts from the east,
    That I may back to Athens by daylight,
    From these that my poor company detest:
    And sleep, that sometimes shuts up sorrow's eye,
    Steal me awhile from mine own company.

Lies down and sleeps

PUCK
    Yet but three? Come one more;
    Two of both kinds make up four.
    Here she comes, curst and sad:
    Cupid is a knavish lad,
    Thus to make poor females mad.

Re-enter HERMIA

HERMIA
    Never so weary, never so in woe,
    Bedabbled with the dew and torn with briers,
    I can no further crawl, no further go;
    My legs can keep no pace with my desires.
    Here will I rest me till the break of day.
    Heavens shield Lysander, if they mean a fray!

Lies down and sleeps

PUCK
    On the ground
    Sleep sound:

I'll apply
To your eye,
Gentle lover, remedy.

Squeezing the juice on LYSANDER's eyes

When thou wakest,
Thou takest
True delight
In the sight
Of thy former lady's eye:
And the country proverb known,
That every man should take his own,
In your waking shall be shown:
Jack shall have Jill;
Nought shall go ill;
The man shall have his mare again, and all shall be well.

Exit

ACT IV

SCENE I.

The same. LYSANDER, DEMETRIUS, HELENA, and HERMIA lying asleep.

Enter TITANIA and BOTTOM; PEASEBLOSSOM, COBWEB, MOTH, MUSTARDSEED, and other Fairies attending; OBERON behind unseen

TITANIA
  Come, sit thee down upon this flowery bed,
  While I thy amiable cheeks do coy,
  And stick musk-roses in thy sleek smooth head,
  And kiss thy fair large ears, my gentle joy.
BOTTOM
  Where's Peaseblossom?
PEASEBLOSSOM
  Ready.
BOTTOM
  Scratch my head Peaseblossom. Where's Mounsieur
  Cobweb?
COBWEB
  Ready.
BOTTOM
  Mounsieur Cobweb, good mounsieur, get you your
  weapons in your hand, and kill me a red-hipped
  humble-bee on the top of a thistle; and, good
  mounsieur, bring me the honey-bag. Do not fret
  yourself too much in the action, mounsieur; and,
  good mounsieur, have a care the honey-bag break not;
  I would be loath to have you overflown with a
  honey-bag, signior. Where's Mounsieur Mustardseed?

MUSTARDSEED

Ready.

BOTTOM

Give me your neaf, Mounsieur Mustardseed. Pray you,
leave your courtesy, good mounsieur.

MUSTARDSEED

What's your Will?

BOTTOM

Nothing, good mounsieur, but to help Cavalery Cobweb
to scratch. I must to the barber's, monsieur; for
methinks I am marvellous hairy about the face; and I
am such a tender ass, if my hair do but tickle me,
I must scratch.

TITANIA

What, wilt thou hear some music,
my sweet love?

BOTTOM

I have a reasonable good ear in music. Let's have
the tongs and the bones.

TITANIA

Or say, sweet love, what thou desirest to eat.

BOTTOM

Truly, a peck of provender: I could munch your good
dry oats. Methinks I have a great desire to a bottle
of hay: good hay, sweet hay, hath no fellow.

TITANIA

I have a venturous fairy that shall seek
The squirrel's hoard, and fetch thee new nuts.

BOTTOM

I had rather have a handful or two of dried peas.
But, I pray you, let none of your people stir me: I
have an exposition of sleep come upon me.

TITANIA

Sleep thou, and I will wind thee in my arms.

Fairies, begone, and be all ways away.

Exeunt fairies

So doth the woodbine the sweet honeysuckle
Gently entwist; the female ivy so
Enrings the barky fingers of the elm.
O, how I love thee! how I dote on thee!

They sleep

Enter PUCK

OBERON
    [Advancing] Welcome, good Robin.
    See'st thou this sweet sight?
    Her dotage now I do begin to pity:
    For, meeting her of late behind the wood,
    Seeking sweet favours from this hateful fool,
    I did upbraid her and fall out with her;
    For she his hairy temples then had rounded
    With a coronet of fresh and fragrant flowers;
    And that same dew, which sometime on the buds
    Was wont to swell like round and orient pearls,
    Stood now within the pretty flowerets' eyes
    Like tears that did their own disgrace bewail.
    When I had at my pleasure taunted her
    And she in mild terms begg'd my patience,
    I then did ask of her her changeling child;
    Which straight she gave me, and her fairy sent
    To bear him to my bower in fairy land.
    And now I have the boy, I will undo
    This hateful imperfection of her eyes:
    And, gentle Puck, take this transformed scalp
    From off the head of this Athenian swain;

68

That, he awaking when the other do,
May all to Athens back again repair
And think no more of this night's accidents
But as the fierce vexation of a dream.
But first I will release the fairy queen.
Be as thou wast wont to be;
See as thou wast wont to see:
Dian's bud o'er Cupid's flower
Hath such force and blessed power.
Now, my Titania; wake you, my sweet queen.

TITANIA
My Oberon! what visions have I seen!
Methought I was enamour'd of an ass.

OBERON
There lies your love.

TITANIA
How came these things to pass?
O, how mine eyes do loathe his visage now!

OBERON
Silence awhile. Robin, take off this head.
Titania, music call; and strike more dead
Than common sleep of all these five the sense.

TITANIA
Music, ho! music, such as charmeth sleep!

Music, still

PUCK
Now, when thou wakest, with thine
own fool's eyes peep.

OBERON
Sound, music! Come, my queen, take hands with me,
And rock the ground whereon these sleepers be.
Now thou and I are new in amity,
And will to-morrow midnight solemnly

Dance in Duke Theseus' house triumphantly,
And bless it to all fair prosperity:
There shall the pairs of faithful lovers be
Wedded, with Theseus, all in jollity.

PUCK

Fairy king, attend, and mark:
I do hear the morning lark.

OBERON

Then, my queen, in silence sad,
Trip we after the night's shade:
We the globe can compass soon,
Swifter than the wandering moon.

TITANIA

Come, my lord, and in our flight
Tell me how it came this night
That I sleeping here was found
With these mortals on the ground.

Exeunt

Horns winded within

Enter THESEUS, HIPPOLYTA, EGEUS, and train

THESEUS

Go, one of you, find out the forester;
For now our observation is perform'd;
And since we have the vaward of the day,
My love shall hear the music of my hounds.
Uncouple in the western valley; let them go:
Dispatch, I say, and find the forester.

Exit an Attendant

We will, fair queen, up to the mountain's top,

And mark the musical confusion
Of hounds and echo in conjunction.

HIPPOLYTA

I was with Hercules and Cadmus once,
When in a wood of Crete they bay'd the bear
With hounds of Sparta: never did I hear
Such gallant chiding: for, besides the groves,
The skies, the fountains, every region near
Seem'd all one mutual cry: I never heard
So musical a discord, such sweet thunder.

THESEUS

My hounds are bred out of the Spartan kind,
So flew'd, so sanded, and their heads are hung
With ears that sweep away the morning dew;
Crook-knee'd, and dew-lapp'd like Thessalian bulls;
Slow in pursuit, but match'd in mouth like bells,
Each under each. A cry more tuneable
Was never holla'd to, nor cheer'd with horn,
In Crete, in Sparta, nor in Thessaly:
Judge when you hear. But, soft! what nymphs are these?

EGEUS

My lord, this is my daughter here asleep;
And this, Lysander; this Demetrius is;
This Helena, old Nedar's Helena:
I wonder of their being here together.

THESEUS

No doubt they rose up early to observe
The rite of May, and hearing our intent,
Came here in grace our solemnity.
But speak, Egeus; is not this the day
That Hermia should give answer of her choice?

EGEUS

It is, my lord.

THESEUS

A Midsummer Night's Dream — Act IV

Go, bid the huntsmen wake them with their horns.

*Horns and shout within. LYSANDER, DEMETRIUS,
HELENA, and HERMIA wake and start up*

Good morrow, friends. Saint Valentine is past:
Begin these wood-birds but to couple now?
LYSANDER
Pardon, my lord.
THESEUS
I pray you all, stand up.
I know you two are rival enemies:
How comes this gentle concord in the world,
That hatred is so far from jealousy,
To sleep by hate, and fear no enmity?
LYSANDER
My lord, I shall reply amazedly,
Half sleep, half waking: but as yet, I swear,
I cannot truly say how I came here;
But, as I think,--for truly would I speak,
And now do I bethink me, so it is,--
I came with Hermia hither: our intent
Was to be gone from Athens, where we might,
Without the peril of the Athenian law.
EGEUS
Enough, enough, my lord; you have enough:
I beg the law, the law, upon his head.
They would have stolen away; they would, Demetrius,
Thereby to have defeated you and me,
You of your wife and me of my consent,
Of my consent that she should be your wife.
DEMETRIUS
My lord, fair Helen told me of their stealth,
Of this their purpose hither to this wood;
And I in fury hither follow'd them,

72

Fair Helena in fancy following me.
But, my good lord, I wot not by what power,--
But by some power it is,--my love to Hermia,
Melted as the snow, seems to me now
As the remembrance of an idle gaud
Which in my childhood I did dote upon;
And all the faith, the virtue of my heart,
The object and the pleasure of mine eye,
Is only Helena. To her, my lord,
Was I betroth'd ere I saw Hermia:
But, like in sickness, did I loathe this food;
But, as in health, come to my natural taste,
Now I do wish it, love it, long for it,
And will for evermore be true to it.

THESEUS
Fair lovers, you are fortunately met:
Of this discourse we more will hear anon.
Egeus, I will overbear your will;
For in the temple by and by with us
These couples shall eternally be knit:
And, for the morning now is something worn,
Our purposed hunting shall be set aside.
Away with us to Athens; three and three,
We'll hold a feast in great solemnity.
Come, Hippolyta.

Exeunt THESEUS, HIPPOLYTA, EGEUS, and train

DEMETRIUS
These things seem small and undistinguishable,

HERMIA
Methinks I see these things with parted eye,
When every thing seems double.

HELENA
So methinks:

And I have found Demetrius like a jewel,
Mine own, and not mine own.
DEMETRIUS
Are you sure
That we are awake? It seems to me
That yet we sleep, we dream. Do not you think
The duke was here, and bid us follow him?
HERMIA
Yea; and my father.
HELENA
And Hippolyta.
LYSANDER
And he did bid us follow to the temple.
DEMETRIUS
Why, then, we are awake: let's follow him
And by the way let us recount our dreams.

Exeunt

BOTTOM
[Awaking] When my cue comes, call me, and I will
answer: my next is, 'Most fair Pyramus.' Heigh-ho!
Peter Quince! Flute, the bellows-mender! Snout,
the tinker! Starveling! God's my life, stolen
hence, and left me asleep! I have had a most rare
vision. I have had a dream, past the wit of man to
say what dream it was: man is but an ass, if he go
about to expound this dream. Methought I was--there
is no man can tell what. Methought I was,--and
methought I had,--but man is but a patched fool, if
he will offer to say what methought I had. The eye
of man hath not heard, the ear of man hath not
seen, man's hand is not able to taste, his tongue
to conceive, nor his heart to report, what my dream
was. I will get Peter Quince to write a ballad of

74

this dream: it shall be called Bottom's Dream,
because it hath no bottom; and I will sing it in the
latter end of a play, before the duke:
peradventure, to make it the more gracious, I shall
sing it at her death.

Exit

SCENE II.

Athens. QUINCE'S house.

Enter QUINCE, FLUTE, SNOUT, and STARVELING

QUINCE

Have you sent to Bottom's house ? is he come home
yet?

STARVELING

He cannot be heard of. Out of doubt he is
transported.

FLUTE

If he come not, then the play is marred: it goes
not forward, doth it?

QUINCE

It is not possible: you have not a man in all
Athens able to discharge Pyramus but he.

FLUTE

No, he hath simply the best wit of any handicraft
man in Athens.

QUINCE

Yea and the best person too; and he is a very
paramour for a sweet voice.

FLUTE

You must say 'paragon:' a paramour is, God bless us,
a thing of naught.

Enter SNUG

SNUG

Masters, the duke is coming from the temple, and
there is two or three lords and ladies more married:
if our sport had gone forward, we had all been made
men.

FLUTE

O sweet bully Bottom! Thus hath he lost sixpence a
day during his life; he could not have 'scaped
sixpence a day: an the duke had not given him
sixpence a day for playing Pyramus, I'll be hanged;
he would have deserved it: sixpence a day in
Pyramus, or nothing.

Enter BOTTOM

BOTTOM

Where are these lads? where are these hearts?

QUINCE

Bottom! O most courageous day! O most happy hour!

BOTTOM

Masters, I am to discourse wonders: but ask me not
what; for if I tell you, I am no true Athenian. I
will tell you every thing, right as it fell out.

QUINCE

Let us hear, sweet Bottom.

BOTTOM

Not a word of me. All that I will tell you is, that
the duke hath dined. Get your apparel together,
good strings to your beards, new ribbons to your
pumps; meet presently at the palace; every man look
o'er his part; for the short and the long is, our
play is preferred. In any case, let Thisby have
clean linen; and let not him that plays the lion

pair his nails, for they shall hang out for the
lion's claws. And, most dear actors, eat no onions
nor garlic, for we are to utter sweet breath; and I
do not doubt but to hear them say, it is a sweet
comedy. No more words: away! go, away!

Exeunt

ACT V

SCENE I.

Athens. The palace of THESEUS.

Enter THESEUS, HIPPOLYTA, PHILOSTRATE, Lords and Attendants

HIPPOLYTA
'Tis strange my Theseus, that these
lovers speak of.

THESEUS
More strange than true: I never may believe
These antique fables, nor these fairy toys.
Lovers and madmen have such seething brains,
Such shaping fantasies, that apprehend
More than cool reason ever comprehends.
The lunatic, the lover and the poet
Are of imagination all compact:
One sees more devils than vast hell can hold,
That is, the madman: the lover, all as frantic,
Sees Helen's beauty in a brow of Egypt:
The poet's eye, in fine frenzy rolling,
Doth glance from heaven to earth, from earth to heaven;
And as imagination bodies forth
The forms of things unknown, the poet's pen
Turns them to shapes and gives to airy nothing
A local habitation and a name.
Such tricks hath strong imagination,
That if it would but apprehend some joy,
It comprehends some bringer of that joy;
Or in the night, imagining some fear,
How easy is a bush supposed a bear!

HIPPOLYTA

But all the story of the night told over,
And all their minds transfigured so together,
More witnesseth than fancy's images
And grows to something of great constancy;
But, howsoever, strange and admirable.

THESEUS

Here come the lovers, full of joy and mirth.

Enter LYSANDER, DEMETRIUS, HERMIA, and HELENA

Joy, gentle friends! joy and fresh days of love
Accompany your hearts!

LYSANDER

More than to us
Wait in your royal walks, your board, your bed!

THESEUS

Come now; what masques, what dances shall we have,
To wear away this long age of three hours
Between our after-supper and bed-time?
Where is our usual manager of mirth?
What revels are in hand? Is there no play,
To ease the anguish of a torturing hour?
Call Philostrate.

PHILOSTRATE

Here, mighty Theseus.

THESEUS

Say, what abridgement have you for this evening?
What masque? what music? How shall we beguile
The lazy time, if not with some delight?

PHILOSTRATE

There is a brief how many sports are ripe:
Make choice of which your highness will see first.

Giving a paper

THESEUS

[Reads] 'The battle with the Centaurs, to be sung
By an Athenian eunuch to the harp.'
We'll none of that: that have I told my love,
In glory of my kinsman Hercules.

Reads

'The riot of the tipsy Bacchanals,
Tearing the Thracian singer in their rage.'
That is an old device; and it was play'd
When I from Thebes came last a conqueror.

Reads

'The thrice three Muses mourning for the death
Of Learning, late deceased in beggary.'
That is some satire, keen and critical,
Not sorting with a nuptial ceremony.

Reads

'A tedious brief scene of young Pyramus
And his love Thisbe; very tragical mirth.'
Merry and tragical! tedious and brief!
That is, hot ice and wondrous strange snow.
How shall we find the concord of this discord?

PHILOSTRATE

A play there is, my lord, some ten words long,
Which is as brief as I have known a play;
But by ten words, my lord, it is too long,
Which makes it tedious; for in all the play
There is not one word apt, one player fitted:
And tragical, my noble lord, it is;
For Pyramus therein doth kill himself.
Which, when I saw rehearsed, I must confess,

Made mine eyes water; but more merry tears
The passion of loud laughter never shed.
THESEUS
What are they that do play it?
PHILOSTRATE
Hard-handed men that work in Athens here,
Which never labour'd in their minds till now,
And now have toil'd their unbreathed memories
With this same play, against your nuptial.
THESEUS
And we will hear it.
PHILOSTRATE
No, my noble lord;
It is not for you: I have heard it over,
And it is nothing, nothing in the world;
Unless you can find sport in their intents,
Extremely stretch'd and conn'd with cruel pain,
To do you service.
THESEUS
I will hear that play;
For never anything can be amiss,
When simpleness and duty tender it.
Go, bring them in: and take your places, ladies.

Exit PHILOSTRATE

HIPPOLYTA
I love not to see wretchedness o'er charged
And duty in his service perishing.
THESEUS
Why, gentle sweet, you shall see no such thing.
HIPPOLYTA
He says they can do nothing in this kind.
THESEUS
The kinder we, to give them thanks for nothing.

81

Our sport shall be to take what they mistake:
And what poor duty cannot do, noble respect
Takes it in might, not merit.
Where I have come, great clerks have purposed
To greet me with premeditated welcomes;
Where I have seen them shiver and look pale,
Make periods in the midst of sentences,
Throttle their practised accent in their fears
And in conclusion dumbly have broke off,
Not paying me a welcome. Trust me, sweet,
Out of this silence yet I pick'd a welcome;
And in the modesty of fearful duty
I read as much as from the rattling tongue
Of saucy and audacious eloquence.
Love, therefore, and tongue-tied simplicity
In least speak most, to my capacity.

Re-enter PHILOSTRATE

PHILOSTRATE
So please your grace, the Prologue is address'd.
THESEUS
Let him approach.

Flourish of trumpets

Enter QUINCE for the Prologue

Prologue
If we offend, it is with our good will.
That you should think, we come not to offend,
But with good will. To show our simple skill,
That is the true beginning of our end.
Consider then we come but in despite.
We do not come as minding to contest you,

82

Our true intent is. All for your delight
We are not here. That you should here repent you,
The actors are at hand and by their show
You shall know all that you are like to know.

THESEUS

This fellow doth not stand upon points.

LYSANDER

He hath rid his prologue like a rough colt; he knows
not the stop. A good moral, my lord: it is not
enough to speak, but to speak true.

HIPPOLYTA

Indeed he hath played on his prologue like a child
on a recorder; a sound, but not in government.

THESEUS

His speech, was like a tangled chain; nothing
impaired, but all disordered. Who is next?

Enter Pyramus and Thisbe, Wall, Moonshine, and Lion

Prologue

Gentles, perchance you wonder at this show;
But wonder on, till truth make all things plain.
This man is Pyramus, if you would know;
This beauteous lady Thisby is certain.
This man, with lime and rough-cast, doth present
Wall, that vile Wall which did these lovers sunder;
And through Wall's chink, poor souls, they are content
To whisper. At the which let no man wonder.
This man, with lanthorn, dog, and bush of thorn,
Presenteth Moonshine; for, if you will know,
By moonshine did these lovers think no scorn
To meet at Ninus' tomb, there, there to woo.
This grisly beast, which Lion hight by name,
The trusty Thisby, coming first by night,
Did scare away, or rather did affright;

And, as she fled, her mantle she did fall,
Which Lion vile with bloody mouth did stain.
Anon comes Pyramus, sweet youth and tall,
And finds his trusty Thisby's mantle slain:
Whereat, with blade, with bloody blameful blade,
He bravely broach'd is boiling bloody breast;
And Thisby, tarrying in mulberry shade,
His dagger drew, and died. For all the rest,
Let Lion, Moonshine, Wall, and lovers twain
At large discourse, while here they do remain.

Exeunt Prologue, Thisbe, Lion, and Moonshine

THESEUS
I wonder if the lion be to speak.
DEMETRIUS
No wonder, my lord: one lion may, when many asses do.
Wall
In this same interlude it doth befall
That I, one Snout by name, present a wall;
And such a wall, as I would have you think,
That had in it a crannied hole or chink,
Through which the lovers, Pyramus and Thisby,
Did whisper often very secretly.
This loam, this rough-cast and this stone doth show
That I am that same wall; the truth is so:
And this the cranny is, right and sinister,
Through which the fearful lovers are to whisper.
THESEUS
Would you desire lime and hair to speak better?
DEMETRIUS
It is the wittiest partition that ever I heard
discourse, my lord.

Enter Pyramus

THESEUS
    Pyramus draws near the wall: silence!
Pyramus
    O grim-look'd night! O night with hue so black!
    O night, which ever art when day is not!
    O night, O night! alack, alack, alack,
    I fear my Thisby's promise is forgot!
    And thou, O wall, O sweet, O lovely wall,
    That stand'st between her father's ground and mine!
    Thou wall, O wall, O sweet and lovely wall,
    Show me thy chink, to blink through with mine eyne!

Wall holds up his fingers

    Thanks, courteous wall: Jove shield thee well for this!
    But what see I? No Thisby do I see.
    O wicked wall, through whom I see no bliss!
    Cursed be thy stones for thus deceiving me!
THESEUS
    The wall, methinks, being sensible, should curse again.
Pyramus
    No, in truth, sir, he should not. 'Deceiving me'
    is Thisby's cue: she is to enter now, and I am to
    spy her through the wall. You shall see, it will
    fall pat as I told you. Yonder she comes.

Enter Thisbe

Thisbe
    O wall, full often hast thou heard my moans,
    For parting my fair Pyramus and me!
    My cherry lips have often kiss'd thy stones,
    Thy stones with lime and hair knit up in thee.
Pyramus

I see a voice: now will I to the chink,
To spy an I can hear my Thisby's face. Thisby!
Thisbe
My love thou art, my love I think.
Pyramus
Think what thou wilt, I am thy lover's grace;
And, like Limander, am I trusty still.
Thisbe
And I like Helen, till the Fates me kill.
Pyramus
Not Shafalus to Procrus was so true.
Thisbe
As Shafalus to Procrus, I to you.
Pyramus
O kiss me through the hole of this vile wall!
Thisbe
I kiss the wall's hole, not your lips at all.
Pyramus
Wilt thou at Ninny's tomb meet me straightway?
Thisbe
'Tide life, 'tide death, I come without delay.

Exeunt Pyramus and Thisbe

Wall
Thus have I, Wall, my part discharged so;
And, being done, thus Wall away doth go.

Exit

THESEUS
Now is the mural down between the two neighbours.
DEMETRIUS
No remedy, my lord, when walls are so wilful to hear
without warning.

HIPPOLYTA

This is the silliest stuff that ever I heard.

THESEUS

The best in this kind are but shadows; and the worst
are no worse, if imagination amend them.

HIPPOLYTA

It must be your imagination then, and not theirs.

THESEUS

If we imagine no worse of them than they of
themselves, they may pass for excellent men. Here
come two noble beasts in, a man and a lion.

Enter Lion and Moonshine

Lion

You, ladies, you, whose gentle hearts do fear
The smallest monstrous mouse that creeps on floor,
May now perchance both quake and tremble here,
When lion rough in wildest rage doth roar.
Then know that I, one Snug the joiner, am
A lion-fell, nor else no lion's dam;
For, if I should as lion come in strife
Into this place, 'twere pity on my life.

THESEUS

A very gentle beast, of a good conscience.

DEMETRIUS

The very best at a beast, my lord, that e'er I saw.

LYSANDER

This lion is a very fox for his valour.

THESEUS

True; and a goose for his discretion.

DEMETRIUS

Not so, my lord; for his valour cannot carry his
discretion; and the fox carries the goose.

THESEUS

His discretion, I am sure, cannot carry his valour;
for the goose carries not the fox. It is well:
leave it to his discretion, and let us listen to the moon.

Moonshine

This lanthorn doth the horned moon present;--

DEMETRIUS

He should have worn the horns on his head.

THESEUS

He is no crescent, and his horns are
invisible within the circumference.

Moonshine

This lanthorn doth the horned moon present;
Myself the man i' the moon do seem to be.

THESEUS

This is the greatest error of all the rest: the man
should be put into the lanthorn. How is it else the
man i' the moon?

DEMETRIUS

He dares not come there for the candle; for, you
see, it is already in snuff.

HIPPOLYTA

I am aweary of this moon: would he would change!

THESEUS

It appears, by his small light of discretion, that
he is in the wane; but yet, in courtesy, in all
reason, we must stay the time.

LYSANDER

Proceed, Moon.

Moonshine

All that I have to say, is, to tell you that the
lanthorn is the moon; I, the man in the moon; this
thorn-bush, my thorn-bush; and this dog, my dog.

DEMETRIUS

Why, all these should be in the lanthorn; for all

these are in the moon. But, silence! here comes Thisbe.

Enter Thisbe

Thisbe
This is old Ninny's tomb. Where is my love?
Lion
[Roaring] Oh--

Thisbe runs off

DEMETRIUS
Well roared, Lion.
THESEUS
Well run, Thisbe.
HIPPOLYTA
Well shone, Moon. Truly, the moon shines with a
good grace.

The Lion shakes Thisbe's mantle, and exit

THESEUS
Well moused, Lion.
LYSANDER
And so the lion vanished.
DEMETRIUS
And then came Pyramus.

Enter Pyramus

Pyramus
Sweet Moon, I thank thee for thy sunny beams;
I thank thee, Moon, for shining now so bright;
For, by thy gracious, golden, glittering gleams,
I trust to take of truest Thisby sight.
But stay, O spite!
But mark, poor knight,

What dreadful dole is here!
Eyes, do you see?
How can it be?
O dainty duck! O dear!
Thy mantle good,
What, stain'd with blood!
Approach, ye Furies fell!
O Fates, come, come,
Cut thread and thrum;
Quail, crush, conclude, and quell!

THESEUS

This passion, and the death of a dear friend, would
go near to make a man look sad.

HIPPOLYTA

Beshrew my heart, but I pity the man.

Pyramus

O wherefore, Nature, didst thou lions frame?
Since lion vile hath here deflower'd my dear:
Which is--no, no--which was the fairest dame
That lived, that loved, that liked, that look'd
with cheer.
Come, tears, confound;
Out, sword, and wound
The pap of Pyramus;
Ay, that left pap,
Where heart doth hop:

Stabs himself

Thus die I, thus, thus, thus.
Now am I dead,
Now am I fled;
My soul is in the sky:
Tongue, lose thy light;
Moon take thy flight:

Exit Moonshine

Now die, die, die, die, die.

Dies

DEMETRIUS
No die, but an ace, for him; for he is but one.
LYSANDER
Less than an ace, man; for he is dead; he is nothing.
THESEUS
With the help of a surgeon he might yet recover, and
prove an ass
HIPPOLYTA
How chance Moonshine is gone before Thisbe comes
back and finds her lover?
THESEUS
She will find him by starlight. Here she comes; and
her passion ends the play.

Re-enter Thisbe

HIPPOLYTA
Methinks she should not use a long one for such a
Pyramus: I hope she will be brief.
DEMETRIUS
A mote will turn the balance, which Pyramus, which
Thisbe, is the better; he for a man, God warrant us;
she for a woman, God bless us.
LYSANDER
She hath spied him already with those sweet eyes.
DEMETRIUS
And thus she means, videlicet:--
Thisbe
Asleep, my love?

What, dead, my dove?
O Pyramus, arise!
Speak, speak. Quite dumb?
Dead, dead? A tomb
Must cover thy sweet eyes.
These My lips,
This cherry nose,
These yellow cowslip cheeks,
Are gone, are gone:
Lovers, make moan:
His eyes were green as leeks.
O Sisters Three,
Come, come to me,
With hands as pale as milk;
Lay them in gore,
Since you have shore
With shears his thread of silk.
Tongue, not a word:
Come, trusty sword;
Come, blade, my breast imbrue:

Stabs herself

And, farewell, friends;
Thus Thisby ends:
Adieu, adieu, adieu.

Dies

THESEUS
Moonshine and Lion are left to bury the dead.
DEMETRIUS
Ay, and Wall too.
BOTTOM
[Starting up] No assure you; the wall is down that

parted their fathers. Will it please you to see the epilogue, or to hear a Bergomask dance between two of our company?

THESEUS

No epilogue, I pray you; for your play needs no excuse. Never excuse; for when the players are all dead, there needs none to be blamed. Marry, if he that writ it had played Pyramus and hanged himself in Thisbe's garter, it would have been a fine tragedy: and so it is, truly; and very notably discharged. But come, your Bergomask: let your epilogue alone.

A dance

The iron tongue of midnight hath told twelve:
Lovers, to bed; 'tis almost fairy time.
I fear we shall out-sleep the coming morn
As much as we this night have overwatch'd.
This palpable-gross play hath well beguiled
The heavy gait of night. Sweet friends, to bed.
A fortnight hold we this solemnity,
In nightly revels and new jollity.

Exeunt

Enter PUCK

PUCK

Now the hungry lion roars,
And the wolf behowls the moon;
Whilst the heavy ploughman snores,
All with weary task fordone.
Now the wasted brands do glow,
Whilst the screech-owl, screeching loud,

Puts the wretch that lies in woe
In remembrance of a shroud.
Now it is the time of night
That the graves all gaping wide,
Every one lets forth his sprite,
In the church-way paths to glide:
And we fairies, that do run
By the triple Hecate's team,
From the presence of the sun,
Following darkness like a dream,
Now are frolic: not a mouse
Shall disturb this hallow'd house:
I am sent with broom before,
To sweep the dust behind the door.

Enter OBERON and TITANIA with their train

OBERON
Through the house give gathering light,
By the dead and drowsy fire:
Every elf and fairy sprite
Hop as light as bird from brier;
And this ditty, after me,
Sing, and dance it trippingly.
TITANIA
First, rehearse your song by rote
To each word a warbling note:
Hand in hand, with fairy grace,
Will we sing, and bless this place.

Song and dance

OBERON
Now, until the break of day,
Through this house each fairy stray.

To the best bride-bed will we,
Which by us shall blessed be;
And the issue there create
Ever shall be fortunate.
So shall all the couples three
Ever true in loving be;
And the blots of Nature's hand
Shall not in their issue stand;
Never mole, hare lip, nor scar,
Nor mark prodigious, such as are
Despised in nativity,
Shall upon their children be.
With this field-dew consecrate,
Every fairy take his gait;
And each several chamber bless,
Through this palace, with sweet peace;
And the owner of it blest
Ever shall in safety rest.
Trip away; make no stay;
Meet me all by break of day.

Exeunt OBERON, TITANIA, and train

PUCK
    If we shadows have offended,
    Think but this, and all is mended,
    That you have but slumber'd here
    While these visions did appear.
    And this weak and idle theme,
    No more yielding but a dream,
    Gentles, do not reprehend:
    if you pardon, we will mend:
    And, as I am an honest Puck,
    If we have unearned luck
    Now to 'scape the serpent's tongue,

A Midsummer Night's Dream – Act V

We will make amends ere long;
Else the Puck a liar call;
So, good night unto you all.
Give me your hands, if we be friends,
And Robin shall restore amends.

The End

Biography

A Short Life of Edward de Vere, 17th Earl of Oxford

by Dr. Kevin Gilvary, President
The de Vere Society

He was born on 12 April 1550 at Castle Hedingham, his family's ancestral home. His father, John de Vere, 16th Earl, was Lord Great Chamberlain and attended the coronations of both Mary and Elizabeth Tudor. His mother was Margaret Golding. Edward was 11 when, in 1561, Queen Elizabeth visited Hedingham for four days of masques, feasting and entertainments. When his father died in 1562, young Oxford left to become, like Bertram in *All's Well that Ends Well*, a ward of the Crown under the guardianship of William Cecil, the Queen's private secretary (later Lord Burghley, Lord Treasurer). His mother married Charles Tyrrell and seems to have passed out of the boy's life. His sister Mary went to live with her stepfather and the siblings were not reunited for some years.

According to a curriculum in Cecil's own hand, Edward de Vere's daily studies included dancing, French, Latin, writing and drawing, cosmography, penmanship, riding, shooting, exercise and prayer. Edward de Vere showed a prodigious talent for scholarship from his early years, and we may ascribe his lifelong love of learning to the influence of two of his early tutors. The first was Sir Thomas Smith who was, perhaps, England's most respected Greek scholar and the former Cambridge tutor of Sir William Cecil. It was, no doubt, through Cecil's influence that Edward de Vere spent some time living in the household of Smith in his early years, during which time he spent about five months at Smith's alma mater, Queens' College, Cambridge. Smith was a scholar of widely varied interests – this was reflected in his 400-volume library, some of which is still extant at Cambridge. De Vere's other tutor was Laurence Nowell, who was not only an accomplished cartographer but was also England's premier scholar of Anglo-Saxon literature – it was Nowell who possessed the only known copy of *Beowulf*.

Another important influence on Edward de Vere's early studies was his maternal uncle Arthur Golding, an officer in the Court of Wards under Cecil, who is credited with the translation of Ovid's *Metamorphoses*, published in 1567, a book widely recognised as having a major influence on 'Shakespeare'.

Following on from his matriculation at Cambridge in November 1558, Edward was awarded an honorary MA by Cambridge during a Royal progress in August 1564, and another degree by Oxford University during a Royal progress in 1566. Edward de Vere then attended Gray's Inn to study law. One notable feature of the Elizabethan Inns of Court was a tradition of mounting dramatic productions and of hosting the various touring companies of players.

In 1570 he served in a military campaign in Scotland under the Earl of Sussex. By 1571, he was reported as a leading luminary of the Court and, for a time, a favourite of Queen Elizabeth. In December 1571 he married Anne Cecil, aged 15, daughter of his guardian. This was a dynastic marriage where all the advantage accrued to Cecil who, ennobled as Baron Burghley, had reduced the social gap between himself and the young Earl.

While Oxford was away on a Grand Tour of Europe, he heard that his daughter Elizabeth Vere had been born in July 1575. On his return in early 1576, he appeared to have been convinced that Elizabeth was not his child; consequently he became estranged from Anne for five years, and exiled himself from Court, taking up residence in the Savoy and concerning himself with literary and musical patronage.

Already, in 1573, *Cardanus Comfort* (the Consolations of Boethius) had been translated from Latin by Thomas Bedingfield and dedicated to Oxford; and published with a preface written by him. In 1576 an anthology, *A Paradise of Daintie Devices*, including several poems by Oxford, was published. These are juvenile works but already show affinities, in both style and thought, with those of the mature Shakespeare.

Oxford's Grand Tour had taken in Paris, Strasbourg, Venice, Genoa, Florence, Palermo and, on his way back through France, Rousillon – the setting for *Love's Labour's Lost*. Oxford spent the best part of a year travelling in Italy in 1576, and becoming involved with moneylenders. He came back to England fluent in Italian and well acquainted with the northern Italian cities, to be satirised by Gabriel Harvey as 'The Italian Earl'. On his way back his ship was attacked by pirates in the English Channel (cf. *Hamlet*). Fourteen of 'Shakespeare's' plays have Italian settings, in which he put his detailed knowledge of the country, beyond pure book knowledge, to good use.

1573 saw the birth of Henry Wriothesley, Earl of Southampton. Although history has not bequeathed to us any evidence of a direct relationship between the two men, in the relatively small world of the royal Court, they must have been acquainted with each other. The poems *Venus and Adonis* (1593) and *The Rape of Lucrece* (1594) were dedicated to Southampton. These were the first works to be published under the name 'Shakespeare' and for the next five years the records show the byline 'Shakespeare' to have been associated exclusively with these two poems. Plays under the name 'Shakespeare' did not appear in print until 1598, the year that Lord Burghley died.

In May 1577 Oxford invested in Frobisher's voyage in the ship *Edward Bonaventure*. Despite its name, the ship's voyage across the Atlantic in search of the North-West Passage lost money; consequently he was forced to sell three estates (cf. Hamlet's words 'I am but mad north-north-west' II.1.). In 1578 he invested in Frobisher's second expedition, which also lost money, forcing further sales of estates.

He was mentioned by Gabriel Harvey in an address to Queen Elizabeth in July 1578, as a prolific private poet and one 'whose countenance shakes spears'. In the same year John Lyly, Oxford's secretary, published *Euphues.The Anatomy of Wit*, followed in 1579 by *Euphues and his England*, dedicated to Oxford. These two books launched the fashion for 'Euphuism', a style characterized by high-flown language, satirized in *Love's Labour's Lost*.

In March 1581 Oxford's mistress, Anne Vavasour, who was one of Queen Elizabeth's Ladies of the Bedchamber, gave birth to a son. The lovers and their son were sent to the Tower by an infuriated Queen but swiftly released (cf. *Measure for Measure*). After his release, Oxford was wounded in a street-fight provoked by Thomas Knyvet, a kinsman of Anne Vavasour; affrays continued in the streets of London between the rival gangs of supporters for over a year (cf.*Romeo and Juliet*).

In December 1581 he resumed living with his long-suffering and devoted wife, and accepted Elizabeth

Vere as his child. Tragically, their only son died one day after his birth. Three more daughters followed, of whom Susan and Bridget survived.

In 1584, Robert Greene's *Gwydonius; the Card of Fancy* was dedicated to him, identifying him as a 'pre-eminent writer'. In 1586, when he was 36, he served on the tribunal which condemned Mary, Queen of Scots to execution.

In the same year, the Queen awarded Oxford an unconditional pension of £1,000 a year for life (about £500,000 at today's value). The motive for this uncharacteristic generosity on the part of the Queen remains a mystery – no accounting was required of Oxford. Her successor, King James I, continued to pay the pension. In reply to Sir Robert Cecil's request that Lord Sheffield's pension be increased, the King refused, saying, 'Great Oxford got no more . . .', leaving us to wonder why Great Oxford? His greatness does not seem to have resided in war or any of the known offices of State. Perhaps a clue can be found in a letter to Burghley, written in 1594, in which Edward de Vere seeks his favour in a matter involving what he describes as 'in mine office' and that this office is beholden to the Queen.

In 1589, George Puttenham published *The Arte of English Poesie* and this contains the most telling recognition of Edward de Vere's literary standing amongst his contemporaries: 'And in her Majesties time that now is are sprong up an other crew of Courtly makers Noble men and Gentlemen of her Majesties owne servantes, who have written excellently well as it would appeare if their doings could be found out and made publicke with the rest, of which number is first that noble Gentleman Edward Earle of Oxford.'

In 1588 his wife Anne, daughter of Lord Burghley, died and in extant letters written at this time, it is reported that Burghley is so incapacitated by grief over the death of his favourite daughter that he is incapable of conducting any Privy Council business.

Three years later, in 1591, Oxford married another of the Queen's Maids of Honour, Elizabeth Trentham, with whom he finally became the father of a male heir; Henry de Vere, 18th Earl of Oxford. Although there is evidence of his continued involvement in Court affairs, from the date of this marriage Edward de Vere's life at his new home at King's Place in Hackney is perhaps the most obscure of his entire life.

In 1594, his ship the *Edward Bonaventure* was wrecked in Bermuda (cf. *The Tempest*). In January 1595, Elizabeth Vere married William Stanley, 6th Earl of Derby, another literary earl who maintained his own company of players – many scholars believe that *A Midsummer Night's Dream* was written for these festivities which were attended by the whole royal Court.

On September 7 1598, Francis Meres' *Palladis Tamia* was registered for publication, naming Oxford as the 'best for comedy'. This is a vital document in Shakespearean history because it includes the first mention of 'Shakespeare' as a playwright, attributing twelve plays to him; until then Shakespeare's reputation had rested on the two narrative poems only.

Oxford suffered all his life from financial difficulties, much of which can be traced to the fact that Queen Elizabeth handed out the bulk of his estate to her favourite courtier the Earl of Leicester during Oxford's minority as a royal ward (estates which Oxford found almost impossible to reclaim), and the ruinous debt she placed upon him over his marriage to Anne Cecil. It is, however, notable that his new brother-in-law, the wealthy Staffordshire landowner and Knight of the Shire Francis Trentham, took over the management of Edward de

Vere's near-bankrupt estate from 1591 and gradually nursed it back to health so that, when Oxford died, all of his massive debts had been cleared.

On the Queen's death in 1603 Oxford wrote eloquently to Sir Robert Cecil, son and heir of Lord Burghley, of his 'great grief'. He wrote, 'In this common shipwreck, mine is above all the rest, who least regarded, though often comforted, she hath left to try my fortune among the alterations of time and chance'.

Oxford died in Hackney in 1604, cause unknown. Parish records state that he was buried in Hackney Church on July 6, but a family history by his first cousin Percival Golding, states 'Edward de Vere ... a man in mind and body absolutely accomplished with honorable endowments ... lieth buried at Westminster'. No record of such a burial can now be traced in Westminster Abbey, where there is a Vere family tomb.

The Aftermath of Oxford's life and death

During the winter season 1604-05, six of Shakespeare's plays were presented at Court by command of King James I. This has an air of commemoration. In 1609 the *Sonnets* were published in a pirated edition. The famous dedication describes the author as 'our ever-living', a phrase invariably used only of the dead.

In 1622 Henry Peacham published, in *The Compleat Gentelman*, a list of poets who made Elizabeth's reign a 'golden age'. Unaccountably, he omitted Shakespeare but placed the Earl of Oxford in first place in his list – perhaps he knew them to be the same person. This is unlike Meres who included them both – maybe one reason was because he didn't know Oxford and Shakespeare were the same person.

We do not know who instigated publication of the First Folio Edition of the Shakespeare plays in 1623, but there is no mention of any executor or relative of Shakspere of Stratford in connection with it. However, of the two brothers who financed it and to whom it was dedicated, one – Philip Earl of Montgomery – was the husband of Oxford's daughter Susan, while the other – William Earl of Pembroke – had once been a suitor for her sister Bridget. Pembroke was Lord Chamberlain, the supreme authority in the world of theatre, and thus in a position to decide which plays were to be published and which suppressed. We also know that Ben Jonson, who wrote much of the introductory material, was an intimate associate of the de Vere family after Oxford's death. The First Folio was therefore very much a family affair, but the family was not the one in Stratford-on-Avon.

An AfterVerse

For those with yet an interest
In strenuous debate
We've compiled a list of books and films
Your appetite to sate.
From this study clear your mind
Of doubt and all misgiving-
Who from us has long since gone
And who is ever-living.

Selected References & Bibliography
About the Author
Edward de Vere, 17th Earl of Oxford

Books

♦ Anderson, M. (2005). *Shakespeare by Another Name: The Life of Edward de Vere, Earl of Oxford, The Man who was Shakespeare.* New York: Gotham Books. *--A physicist by training with research interest in how evidence supports or negates a theory, Mark Anderson spent ten years investigating Edward de Vere as the author of Shake-speare's works.*

♦Farina, William. (2006). *De Vere as Shakespeare: An Oxfordian Reading of the Canon.* Jefferson, NC. McFarland & Company.

--Each of the plays and poems is individually assessed and explored in its own chapter, using the innumerable connections between the text itself and the life of its author, Edward de Vere.

♦ Looney, J. Thomas (2018). *Shakespeare Identified.* Cary, N.C. Veritas Publicaations.
--First published in 1920 this book began the modern Oxfordian movement. From reading it, Sigmund Freud became convinced and John Galsworthy called it "the best detective story I ever read."

♦ Ogburn, C. (1992). *The Mysterious William Shakespeare.* McLean (Va.): EPM.
--An in depth exploration and must read foundational book on the authorship question.

♦Sobran, Joseph. (1997). *Alias Shakespeare: Solving the Greatest Literary Mystery of All Time.* New York; The Free Press, A Division of Simon & Schuster.
--A concise exploration of the puzzling questions surrounding the authorship controversy with the evidence decisively supporting the case for Edward de Vere, the 17th Earl of Oxford, as the rightful author of the Shakespeare plays and poems.

♦Whittemore, Hank. (2016), *100 Reasons Shake-speare Was the Earl of Oxford.* Somerville MA. Forever Press.
►Also with further discussion and public comment at: *Hank Whittemore's Shakespeare Blog.*
https://hankwhittemore.com/
--In both the book and online blog cited above, Whittemore presents a concise introduction to the

authorship question that examines 100 different aspects, from biographical and historical records, that point to Edward de Vere as the true writer of the Shake-speare plays and poems.

Websites & Videos

▶ De Vere Society. (2019). The de Vere Society – Dedicated to the proposition that the works of Shakespeare were written by Edward de Vere, 17th Earl of Oxford. [online] Deveresociety.co.uk. Available at: https://deveresociety.co.uk
--A very complete resource with substantial biographical and authorship information and links.

▶ The Oxford Fellowship (2019). Shakespeare Oxford Fellowship | Research and Discussion of the Shakespeare Authorship Question. [online] Shakespeare Oxford Fellowship. Available at: https://shakespeareoxfordfellowship.org/
--A seminal online resource especially focusing on the authorship question.

▶ Waugh, A. (2019). Alexander Waugh. [online] YouTube. Available at: https://www.youtube.com/channel/UCHN7SCKlsa9lPYJ mqqQ2uIg/featured/
OR simply search: 'Alexander Waugh'
--Alexander Waugh is a leading authorship scholar who has produced many fascinating video presentations on the authorship question. This link is to his YouTube Channel.

▶ Columbia Pictures & Centropolis Entertainment. (2011). *Anonymous*. Produced and directed by Roland Emmerich. [DVD]
--This mainstream film is both entertaining and enlightening. It presents a superb dramatization of the character of Edward de Vere, setting out in detail the historical and personal context which made his anonymous authorship necessary.

▶Centropolis Entertainment and First Folio Pictures. *Last Will and Testament.* (2012). [DVD]
--A thoughtful and ground-breaking video documentary introduction to the Shakespeare authorship question.

Acknowledgment
Our sincere thanks to
The de Vere Society
and
The Shakespeare Oxford Fellowship
for their inspiration, help and support
in creating this series.

Attributions
--Character list from Wikipedia under
the Creative Commons License 3.0
--Play text from the Moby(tm) editions
in the public domain

Photos
Coat of Arms of Edward de Vere
Source: Wikimedia.org
Author: George Baker / Public domain

The Keep at Castle Hedingham
Source: geograph.org.uk
Author: David Phillips / CC BY-SA 2.0

The de Vere Family Coat of Arms
Source: Wikimedia
Author: Rs-nourse / CC BY-SA 3.0
(https://creativecommons.org/licenses/by-sa/3.0)

View from The Minstrels' Gallery, Hedingham Castle
Source: geograph.org.uk/p/3162585
Photo by: © PAUL FARMER - cc-by-sa/2.0

Cover/Inside: The Welbeck portrait of Edward de Vere (1575). Artist unknown. National Portrait Gallery, London.

This work has been edited and produced by

Verus Publishing
www.verusbooks.com

V | P

www.ingramcontent.com/pod-product-compliance
Lightning Source LLC
Chambersburg PA
CBHW030420100426
42812CB00028B/3041/J